THE PRISONERS OF SIRIUS

THE PRISONERS OF SIRIUS

Book interior layout design:
Shabbir Hussain, access Ideas@yahoo.com

CONTENTS

PROLOGUE

In contending with life's challenges, we struggle every day; we fight every new odd and fear that constantly pushes us towards the end: death. Why are people afraid of death itself? It is understandable to fear the agony that may come in those last moments, but why fear what lies beyond? Is it because they believe there is no going back, meaning no chance to right the wrongs we have done in life? Or is it because no one can know what awaits them after death? Or if they come back in some way?

They do, but we just don't realize it.

There comes a time when you feel a strong attachment to someone you have just met, but you cannot explain why. For this connection to be so powerful, our souls must have crossed paths before because we are able to bond without reason. We are repaying the karmic debt from our past lives, even if it is painful; this soul we meet may have entered our life for revenge, it reminds us, even if we do not remember it. The Creator does not want souls to be indebted to each other because every encounter has a reason; everything is recorded, and we have a destiny to fulfill.

After death, good people go to heaven and bad people go to hell. However, when you realize that you have karma, you know that whatever you do in life, good or bad, you will have to face the consequences in death. Death is an opportunity to return to life's cycle and correct the mistakes we have made. The world may be heaven to some people and hell to others. What then is there to fear of death?

Our body may belong to us, but what about our soul? Does it also belong to us? Temporarily, yes, but after death, the body decays and eventually returns to dust. And what is a soul exactly? It is a singular cosmic entity that is hard to describe. It is the eruption of presence behind the wolf's howl at the moon. It is the reason we bask in the picturesque synchronicity of life's fated moments, like being captured by the beckoning beauty of a quiet sunset or feeling the vast nothingness of space on a shimmering night. Our souls sustain in whatever form we may take, here or in the future. What a strange feeling to live in another body or something as insignificant as a grain of salt.

CHAPTER ONE

THE FINAL HOURS

It was a Tuesday, and just like any other day, the rain fell heavily in London. Pedestrians hurried, huddled beneath umbrellas, seeking shelter wherever they could. Some of them headed for the nearest underground station, mumbling apologies as they brushed past each other, while others shoved their way through without courtesy. They gathered at bus stops, like the one near the Royal London Hospital, exchanging nods of acknowledgement with fellow would-be passengers and engaging in small talk, mostly about the inclement weather. Most waited in silence as traffic moved slowly, coming to a halt, and starting again at traffic lights, without end.

Somewhere in the city, the blaring sirens of emergency vehicles were even louder than the rumble of engines, but even they were still just a part of daily life in the bustling metropolis. However, inside the hospital, many were unaware of what was happening outside. Some of them would never be aware again.

Isabella had been involved in a major car accident a few days prior, leaving her with severe injuries. She had been taken to the nearest hospital, where doctors had done everything, they could save her, but they knew she had a tough battle ahead. While they had managed to address the damage to her vital organs, her head injury had left them with little choice but to keep her in a coma, allowing the swelling in her brain to subside. Time and hope were all they could offer now, and they could do little more than watch, wait, and pray.

Suddenly, without warning and with no change in the sound from the monitors at the side of her bed, she opened her eyes. She felt a moment of panic as she tried to understand her surroundings, unable to remember what had happened or where she was. Sliding out of bed, she stood up, feeling strangely light, with her feet barely touching the floor.

She turned to the bed, expecting to see rumpled sheets and a pillow still indented by the weight of her head. Instead, she saw herself still lying there, connected to tubes and wires, with machines flashing and beeping. This only added to her confusion. If she was awake and standing, then whose body was on the bed? Who was this other woman who looked just like her?

A doctor entered unannounced; the door swung closed behind him. He was a tall man, dressed in green operating theatre scrubs, his face drawn and tired, his eyes focused solely on the bed. Isabella called out to him, but he neither saw nor heard her. He was completely engrossed with the body on the bed. He checked the machines, made a note on the clipboard at the bottom of the bed; his movements were dutiful, almost rehearsed, and his expression remained placid as he moved about. He left quickly without uttering a word.

Isabella couldn't comprehend what was happening—the body on the bed was hers, being sustained by machines; they were forcing air into her lungs, pumping blood through her body. The realization crept upon her like a million icy needles crawling over her heart, which was strange because although her current presence had no tangible weight, she could feel her core, the nexus of her consciousness. That was her in that bed, and this was still her standing beside her own body—which could only mean one thing. At that moment, a dazzling light shone through the previously grey and rain-streaked window, filling the room with brightness before gradually taking on the familiar shape of her father.

Isabella had been 37 years old when her father passed away almost three years before. The grief she felt had sent her into a spiral of depression she thought she would never escape. It had been a time when she had needed him more than ever, but he was no longer there. Perhaps if she had sought help during those terrible lows, by finding someone else who might have been able to help her, she might have had more tranquility in her life.

"Daddy, how did you get here? I don't understand. Is this real, or am I dreaming?" She threw her arms around her father and hugged him, holding him tight. "I'm so confused, I don't understand what's happening." She released her hold on him, just so she could look into his eyes.

Her father said nothing. He just smiled and held Isabella's hand tenderly, leading her to where the window had been. Instead of a window, it was now the entrance to a tunnel, leading them away from the room, away from the beeps and flashing lights of the machines, away from the body lying on the bed. A brilliant white light beckoned to them from the far end, and Isabella offered no resistance. There was a feeling of urgency and uncertainty as she left everything behind—everything she had ever known, with no idea of whether she would return.

Isabella didn't feel like she was walking; she was almost floating, passing through this dark and almost formless tunnel towards the dazzling light that slowly drew closer, ushering in a beautiful and tender breeze that brushed her skin. The gentleness of that wind had a calming effect, easing her fear and giving her a sense of peace.

Gradually, the light began to fade, and Isabella squeezed her father's hand tightly before they suddenly stopped in a large, but magnificent hall. The vast room was dimly lit, and the source of illumination was unclear, making it feel colder and somehow disturbing. The walls of the room were covered in a deep, twisting purple, as if it were the very fabric of the walls, contorting and flowing. The only source of illumination came from a glorious dome above, but its exact origin remained unclear, adding to the chilling and unsettling atmosphere. Her father simply smiled, as if to reassure her that there was nothing to worry about.

He gestured towards a burgundy-colored armchair on the right side of the room. It was the only object bathed in a pool of light brighter than its surroundings. Bewildered, she obeyed. She scanned the dome-ceilinged room with paneled walls adorned with iridescent flower patterns. Above her, the glassy ceiling rose high, beyond the reach of sight, leaving a mystery as thick as a cloud. The rest of the room offered no answers as to why she was there. Except for the beautiful patterns on the walls and the floors that gleamed like dark obsidian, she was left in the dark, looking to her father for clarity.

As she sat in the chair, it adjusted to fit her, resizing itself, with its arms bending inward to trap her in a tight embrace, until she could no longer stand up. She struggled against the restraint, but it made no difference. She was almost paralyzed, only able to move her hands and head—thankfully, her hands had not been trapped by the chair. Now, her curiosity turned to fear, and she found herself beginning to cry.

Lost in her despair, Isabella noticed that her father had moved further away from her.

"Calm down, Isabella, everything will be alright," his lips didn't move, his voice only echoed inside her head, as if they shared a joint consciousness. Then he slipped into the shadows, and she was alone. She could no longer see him, but she was sure that he was still there—like he had always been. After her father's death, she had always felt a small inkling suggesting that he was somewhere in proximity, just beyond her reach.

"Spirits communicate with each other through emotions or signals," she thought. The thought floated in from nowhere and made sense to her. It had to be something she knew, something she had learned, something she had read somewhere, or something someone had said. It was something her father was trying to tell her at that moment. "This is the afterlife; you are no longer in the real world." As she willed herself to accept, she tried to make sense of it all. Death might be the end of one life, but it marks the beginning of a new one.

CHAPTER TWO

THE COURT HALL

"THE JUDGE'S JUSTICE SHOULD PREVAIL OVER HIS LOVE AND MERCY"

The Court Hall

Isabella's soul awaited judgment on her life now that it was over, although she had been aware of it. The room she was in served as the courtroom, where matters were settled by the Great Judge Sirius. On this occasion, the court had convened not only for Isabella, but there was also another soul to be judged that day: his name was Theo.

How strange it was that, as in life, the moment of death sometimes brought people together. Theo had died barely seven minutes after Isabella, but apart from this coincidence of timing, what had brought them to this place together?

Theo had been preparing for his fortieth birthday. He had meticulously planned every detail, determined to make it perfect. However, life always had its own plans. Sometimes he wondered how fortunate he had been to achieve what he had. It may not have been the career he had once dreamed of, but he had still attained the lifestyle he desired. He worked hard, and it had been a long time since he last worried about paying his bills or having enough in his bank account for groceries at the supermarket checkout.

He had founded an interior décor and refurbishment company for luxury hotels and houses, which had exceeded his initial ambitions. He had put in relentless effort to ensure its success and made changes in his life whenever he felt something was holding him back or causing unhappiness. Business and his own happiness were the most important things to him, and nothing would stand in his way. Not even his family.

His marriage had been challenging at times, more difficult than he was willing to accept, and eventually he had chosen to walk away from it, leaving his wife, Martha, alone with their young son. Her cancer diagnosis and treatment had added strain to their relationship, increasing the demands on his time and prolonging arguments that had no resolution. She wanted him to work less, to spend more time at home and help with their son. She didn't understand that he couldn't slow down because doing so would cause things to unravel. Without him, the business would fail, and without the business, he feared he might also crumble.

There wasn't enough space in his life for any of this, and eventually he reached a breaking point, leaving him with no choice but to walk away. Even now, despite the passing years, he still felt a twinge of annoyance whenever he thought of them. He knew it was for the best if he didn't think about them at all.

Usually, he could resolve a problem with a swift decision and leave it all behind, never looking back, as if it had never happened.

Theo's son, Jacob, was now 17 and despised him, but he undeniably loved his mother. Unfortunately, life had led Jacob into a downward spiral of drug addiction, leaving him with no means of escape. The last time Theo had spoken to him, Jacob had come begging for money, supposedly to pay for his mother's treatment. Theo had refused, giving the matter no more than a passing thought.

"Isn't the National Health Service good enough for her?" he had said, as if it held the answer to everything.

"Isn't that what I pay my taxes for?" The sentiment could have been lifted from a Charles Dickens novel, yet he meant every word of it.

He wasn't sure if that really was the intention for the money, or if it was meant to feed Jacob's habit, and he didn't really care. The answer remained the same. His final words to his son were, "Don't bother me again. You have nothing to do with me anymore."

He knew it was cruel and unfair, but it needed to be done to put an end to the matter. After all, it was what he had been thinking, and there was little point in sugar-coating it. He justified himself by recalling the bad memories of his time with Martha, all the arguments they had about him not making enough time for her and her unreasonable demands, to convince himself that she deserved it. She wasn't the first woman to treat him like that, but he was determined that she would be the last.

Theo didn't care about fatherhood or Jacob, so the matter didn't upset him. What was in the past should remain in the past; it had nothing to do with the present. It was the best way, the only way.

Barely four months after leaving his family to start a new life, he had fallen in love with an adventurous and beautiful young woman named Gilia, a waiter in the small Italian café opposite his office. She was 15 years his junior but so full of life, everything Martha hadn't been. Theo had been captivated by her beauty and self-assured demeanor, feeling an irresistible attraction towards her. He questioned how he could have possibly fallen in love with someone so deeply, how she could consume his every waking moment and distract him from other important things.

His best friend, Harry, asked how he had become so infatuated with someone. It wasn't the first time Theo had been asked this question, and he suspected it wouldn't be the last.

"Maybe," Theo said, "once in every man's life, there comes a woman who changes everything. Someone who turns everything upside down and makes you see the world in a different light."

"Is that what she's done?" Harry asked. "Has she turned your life upside down? It's a slippery slope."

"Slippery slope? What are you talking about?"

"Before you know it, you'll be leaving a manager in charge of the business so you can spend more time with her. You'll end up having someone else making important decisions, decisions you might not have made. The wrong decisions. Who will you blame? Will it be the manager's fault? Or will it be yours for not being there to make them yourself? Or maybe you'll end up blaming her."

"That's never going to happen," Theo said.

"You think? I've seen it happen to plenty of people, and it'll happen to you if you let it."

"Then I won't let it. I still know how to keep my personal life and business separate."

His friend made a sound that was half laugh, half grunt, clearly not believing him. It angered Theo, but he didn't rise to it. He was determined to prove that it was possible to have both, even if it meant spending less time with people like Harry.

Years passed, and before long, Theo and Gilia had established a home together and were married. What he hadn't realized was that Gilia had married Theo solely for his money, for the security and lifestyle he could provide. She felt no affection for him; it had all been an act to get what she wanted.

On Theo's birthday, Gilia had prepared a surprise for him, although he had suspected she had something in mind. He didn't want his plans to interfere with whatever she had planned. However, before he left the office for the day, he used his phone to check for any emails that might have arrived late that afternoon. Normally, Theo would have waited until the following morning when his PA would be in the office to manage anything that needed attention. It was a coincidence that he happened to stay late to check them on that particular day.

But coincidence is simply a matter of fate toying with you; everything is planned. God wants you to communicate with him through prayer and provides you with opportunities to change your destiny. He makes you consider events and people to understand the message your soul needs to receive at that moment. While it may be possible to choose your own destiny, it is only the case if you have experienced a spiritual awakening.

One email came from an address Theo didn't recognize, but he opened it to find a series of images attached: He saw Nicholas, his business partner, kissing a woman—and this woman bore a striking resemblance to Gilia. An icicle slipped down Theo's back, and a clammy cold sweat broke out on his palms. Theo shook his head in disbelief, but his will was already guiding him to zoom in. It was Gilia. Nicholas was kissing Gilia! A tremble began in his chest, then echoed through his hands, legs, and breaths. In moments like these, when suddenly shocked by something devastating, the body's senses begin to glitch a bit, and for Theo, it was a sudden weakness, a sudden weight in his arms and legs, and a bit of blurriness in his sight. But even his mind was too distracted by his realization to understand that his blood pressure had shot up.

Gilia's name flashed on his phone screen; she was calling him, but her once warm smile sparked rage in Theo's heart. Without answering, Theo rushed straight to his car and quickly drove home, filled with anger and disappointment. No one had ever deceived him, no one had cheated on him, and now it felt like the foundations of his world were falling apart.

When he arrived home, he went inside feeling more than a little disoriented and found Gilia squeezing orange juice in the kitchen.

"Why didn't you answer your phone?" she snapped angrily. "I called you several times, but you didn't pick up."

Instead of answering, Theo held up his phone to her face, showing her one of the incriminating pictures. Gilia fell silent, her jaw slacked, and acted as if it was nothing. That response was the final blow, and in that moment, Theo knew it had all been a charade. Gilia, on the other hand, continued to squeeze the oranges, but Theo suspected she was just stalling, trying to come up with an explanation she thought he would believe.

"What the hell is going on?" Theo demanded, and within moments, they were shouting at each other, hurling insults and accusations that must have been brewing for some time.

Their voices grew louder and louder, the anger and hurt intensifying, but neither of them was truly listening to the other, not interested in anything the other had to say. Theo suddenly felt hot and sweaty, and a pain shot up his arm before he fell to the ground, clutching his chest. It was enough to startle Gilia, but it didn't change the way she felt. There was still a raging anger inside her that showed no sign of subsiding.

Theo didn't even feel himself fall; he just felt as if an iron vice had grabbed his heart and he was holding on for dear life by a thread. He saw Gilia through bloodshot vision; she stood there, with an orange casually raised to her lips, like a being far beyond his reach. Theo wanted to beg her for help, but he couldn't form the words amidst the pain and the hitching breaths in his lungs. Gilia pretended not to notice, even as he stretched out a flailing arm.

Eventually, he fell silent, his arms still clutching his chest, his features frozen in agony. Only then, when she was certain that it would be too late to save him, did she call for an ambulance. She had already concocted a story about how she had been upstairs, cleaning the bathroom when he arrived home from work, and when she came downstairs, she found him in this state. In the end, she hadn't really needed it. She spluttered her story to the paramedics, but they were more concerned with trying to save Theo, even though they must have known they hadn't been called soon enough.

By the time they got him to the hospital, it was far too late. Theo's final spark of life had slipped away. Gilia shed crocodile tears in front of the doctors when they informed her that they had done everything they could. But God saw everything, and she couldn't deceive Him, even if the doctors were taken in.

Theo had grown up in poverty. Most of the people around him had been in the same position, so the odds were stacked against him. There was no well-to-do extended relative who would swoop in and save the day or provide a springboard for Theo to use to his advantage. It also made his glaring disadvantage indisputable when he compared himself to other kids from better homes with better lives.

Still, Theo never kept his gaze down. He desired a life more like the ones he saw on TV, a better life than what he could see or what appeared logically attainable given his status, and he didn't care what he had to do to achieve it.

Although he had become wealthy over time and wanted to enjoy it to the fullest, he never for a moment thought that there would be a price to pay or that money could not secure him happiness. Somehow, life had brought him Gilia, and although all his dreams seemed to have come true, his happiness didn't last long. The price for what he had done in life was very heavy, and it needed to be paid.

Now, in death, Theo was experiencing the same range of emotions as Isabella. He saw the frenzied animation of the doctors and Gilia's desperate attempts to resurrect his lifeless body on a hospital gurney. He witnessed Gilia's profuse act of sorrow and wondered how he had been so blind. A doctor led her away from the ER, and she stood in the doorway sobbing until no one paid attention to her, then she just slumped down on a nearby bench, exhausted from the day's events. In the ER, Theo stood amidst the chaotic orchestra of desperate efforts to save his life. He watched his body jerk upwards with every shock from the defibrillators, and although he couldn't hear their frantic calls, he found meaning in their animated expressions. Theo was the only abstract part of this scene, standing as a spectator on the outside of color as everything unfolded.

It all climaxed and then everything descended to normal. Theo watched the machines and monitors beep from fast to slow to flatline and watched them slowly but methodically detached wires and tubes from his body.

His mother, whom he had lost four years before, entered the room—it was more like she had diffused into appearance in a whiff of smoke. Although he was touched and surprised when he saw her, an emotion he had rarely felt in life, he did not show it. There was a moment of confusion, but then he realized that he would have to go with her. There was nothing left for him in that room.

"Where are we going?" he asked.

His mother replied sternly, in a voice he remembered all too well, a voice that had rebuked him so often, "You'll see when we get there."

His mother had suffered from a psychological condition, a condition she had inherited from her own mother, and her influence was behind every wrong decision he had ever made in his life. She had always been able to make him do whatever she wanted, no matter how wrong he knew it to be. He had always wanted to please her, no matter how poorly he treated her.

She gestured towards an open void, resembling a cavity in the ordinary plain, as if something had been rolled back to reveal a dark opening. His mother stepped through, and Theo followed behind her, strangely trusting her, as if he were being drawn by some unseen force. As soon as he stepped through, everything changed into a thick fog, and the doorway back to the real world had disappeared.

His mother walked in a straight line ahead of him, and Theo followed her, unable to see beyond her except for her presence. But he knew that the path they walked was a conduit, like a dark tunnel leading somewhere. It was an inexplicable revelation that came naturally to him, as if he had walked this path once before.

Eventually, they emerged into a vast dimly lit courtroom. There was no one in sight, but Theo could sense the presence of witnesses, beings watching just beyond the limits of his vision. No one spoke, but the atmosphere impressed upon him a spaciousness far beyond what he could perceive. The only source of light emanated from the center of the room, where an overhead spotlight illuminated a chair that awaited him.

His mother gestured for him to approach it, but she made no move to follow. He glanced at his mother, seeking reassurance, but she had already vanished, leaving him alone once again.

Theo took a moment to evaluate. If he was being led here and this was some part of the afterlife, then sitting there would signify the completion of his journey. So, he took his place and waited. Unbeknownst to him, he was not alone in this vast room; Isabella was seated opposite him. However, the two souls could not perceive each other, as an unseen barrier rendered them invisible to one another.

After a brief silence, the lighting in the room gradually intensified, sufficiently illuminating the courtroom. It revealed glossy dark floors with an iridescent brilliance reminiscent of obsidian, and magnificent columns reaching towards an unseen ceiling. Each column displayed intricate patterns in an unfamiliar language, and the floors were so smooth that they reflected the surroundings. The room's overall decor exuded a burgundy hue, interwoven with the darkness of the floors. The walls appeared alive, contorting, and curdling as they extended towards an unpredictable ceiling. But the most awe-inspiring aspect was the immense size of the space, seemingly stretching endlessly. The tunnel through which Isabella had entered now appeared distant, and it was impossible to ascertain the true magnitude of the room. Additionally, the two souls could not recall having walked such a great distance from their respective entrances; the physical parameters did not align. This indicated that the room had expanded imperceptibly to their senses.

Despite remaining hidden from each other, the two souls could take in every other aspect of the magnificent hall.

Behind Isabella, two figures dressed in light brown cloaks with hoods drawn over their heads approached a desk with two seats behind it. Isabella was taken aback by this sudden appearance, how the figures and their seats seemed to materialize out of thin air right before her eyes. Their faces, initially obscured in the darkness of their hoods, gradually became visible in the light. They possessed featureless round faces that observed intently. Isabella started to feel fear, but a disconcerting calmness washed over her. One of the figures seemed familiar, not due to any distinct appearance, but rather a vague sensation that it could be her father. She attempted to address him, but the figure raised a finger to where its lips should have been, gesturing for her to remain silent.

On the table in front of the figure, there were several glass vessels, each containing shiny, sparkling dust of different colors. The figure poured some green dust from one of the jars into the palm of its hand and tossed it before the desk. In the blink of an eye, the dust dissipated into nothingness, but simultaneously, the figure's face shifted and contorted, akin to clay being molded, until Isabella found herself staring in horror at her own face. It was as if Isabella had split into two, save for the creature's height.

Similarly, the figure poured some sky-blue powder from a second jar and threw it, speaking in Isabella's own voice, "I was surprised."

Isabella screamed. The figure's face melted like a wax candle placed too close to a fire, returning to its blank and featureless appearance before sitting down. In an instant, Isabella felt a profound sense of weakness, as if all her strength had been drained away. So much was unfolding around her, and she had no inkling of what any of it meant or what would happen next.

CHAPTER THREE

THE MYSTERIOUS JUDGE

♀

Theo remained restrained in his movements within the chair, though his expression did not openly reveal his emotions as Isabella's had. He too had just witnessed the unsettling transformation of the figures seated next to him, and he also sensed his mother's presence within one of them. The figure's face had morphed to mimic his own, and then it spoke in a voice that bore a striking resemblance to his own. Theo attempted to reason with it logically, searching for a recorder somewhere or convincing himself that this was likely a nightmare he would wake up from later. However, given everything he had witnessed thus far, his certainty wavered.

As the abrupt noises of the procedural rites gave way to stillness once more, a brief silence preceded a low hum. Theo and Isabella heard the sound and felt it resonating within them, as if they were contained within the source emitting the sound. It continued to build, growing louder until both souls could sense vibrations emanating from the floors beneath them. Without warning, the floor collapsed just before them! A vicious snarl remained, akin to a gaping mouth that had devoured what was present, leaving behind a pitch-black chasm that emitted loud groans and tremors, shaking the very foundations of the room, and leaving both souls bewildered with fear.

The crash soon subsided, replaced by a harmonious tinkling sound reminiscent of a million glass shards colliding in harmony. Soon enough, that notion was confirmed as glass crystals emerged from the chasm, swirling, and scattering throughout the room at high speed, converging and dispersing in a coordinated spiral that extended far into the indeterminate ceiling. It continued as a steady stream until all those rhythmic oscillations coalesced above, and the glass transmuted into droplets that steadily dripped into the opening. At first, the dripping was slow from the center of the levitated pool, but soon a steady stream poured forth, filling the chasm, and creating a silvery pool.

The pool's surface, smooth and glossy, was disrupted by small ripples, and from its center, tiny dazzling crystals shot into the air like a fountain. Both souls were left speechless, captivated by this spectacle, even as a section of the floor on the far side of the pool elevated to form a raised platform. Soft, warm light illuminated the stage from four different angles, resembling spotlights and leaving the edges of the room in darkness. Everything was in place.

The figures behind the two souls rose to their feet, hands clasped in front of them, yet they remained silent. Both Theo and Isabella felt an urge to stand as well, but the chairs refused to release their restraints, keeping them firmly in place.

Suddenly, the lights in the hall went out, leaving only the faint radiance emanating from the floating crystals above the pool. Like the entrance of a character onto a stage, the radiance gradually intensified, diffusing light throughout the expansive space as the crystals seemed to ascend, converging to form a breathtaking nexus of blinding light. Theo and Isabella could only avert their gaze momentarily. As they returned their focus, they beheld a luminous, large sphere of iridescent beauty. Its exact nature and color were difficult to discern, as its form shimmered with ever-shifting hues. The sphere floated toward the stage, surrounded by a halo of light.

Isabella and Theo experienced an unexpected and profound surge of love, filling them with joy and contentment. Simultaneously, enlightenment dawned upon them, and they realized that this was what the hooded figures had been anticipating.

The pair received a warm yet stern greeting from a voice. "Welcome to the Court of Judgment. I am the spirit of Sirius, and I have been appointed to preside over your case today." The words were followed by another wave of immeasurable unspoken love exchanged between the souls and the Judge.

Somehow, the voice sounded remarkably familiar, but neither Theo nor Isabella could identify to whom it belonged. All they knew was that they placed absolute trust in it, and both were certain that they had heard it before, though they couldn't recall when or where. Without hesitation, they left behind all their worries and fears, now knowing that they were in a safe place.

The lifelines of the two souls intersected, their paths overlapping, leaving a mark on each other's lives.

This was why the court was holding the proceedings for two separate souls simultaneously. They were soul mates, but fate had separated them in life, even though they were now reunited in death.

Occasionally, there are fleeting moments, as slight as a smile across a crowded room when eyes meet and nothing more. Sometimes, there is an unsettling passion during the first encounter between strangers, a feeling that initially seems everlasting but is extinguished far too soon. These chance encounters are often forgotten, only to be partially remembered years later, with an indelible impression.

There is a reason why God removes the person who gave you this beautiful feeling. He sees what we cannot see in that moment, he hears what we cannot hear, or refuses to hear. He wants you to prioritize valuing yourself because He created you as someone worthy of love. You are in danger of being engulfed in a love that will hurt you.

It may initially seem like a punishment, but there are lessons he wants to impart. Sometimes, souls make each other experience this pain because they meet at the wrong time. When you fall in love with God, you contemplate how he created this feeling, and your love for him grows even stronger.

Everyone is accountable for their own actions in life: their decisions, deeds, and words. However, at times, these actions and words are influenced by past traumatic experiences and the fear of repeating them.

These events and people can impact your choices, leading you blindly down the wrong path, causing more mistakes, and missing the correct turns and directions. Eventually, you become utterly lost, surrounded by wicked individuals, and overwhelmed by the consequences of immoral events. You will be held responsible for all the ignored signs, misconduct, and choices you make. Everything will be unveiled in this fair court where wealth, status, and all other worldly matters will be left behind. Your expensive attire, insincere smiles, and foolish ambitions will be stripped away. In life, a person who commits murder must stand trial, give testimony, and face punishment. However, someone who breaks your heart, stealing the light from your life and slowly causing you pain every time you relive the moment, doesn't undergo such a trial, or receive a sentence. For a while, this offender remains unpunished, inflicting suffering on others until they finally face their own day of judgment. Then they won't be able to evade the charges that will be brought against them.

On this day, the wrongdoer will be held accountable for their actions. They will expose their innermost thoughts and face the consequences in the divine court. The truth will be laid bare because the Judge knows all; the Judge is present in your mind when thoughts are conceived.

Theo and Isabella remained motionless in their chairs, their focus fixed on the Judge, awaiting his further words.

The silence was eventually shattered by the voice of the Judge. "I am pleased to see both of you," he said. His words were accompanied by the removal of the invisible screen that had separated Theo and Isabella, allowing them to see each other for the first time in that realm.

Neither of them had anticipated this encounter, witnessing each other after many years. Isabella stared intently at Theo, initially disbelieving that it was the same distasteful man from her past who shared this peculiar moment with her. She observed him for a moment, half-expecting him to transform into one of those figures. Yet Theo remained seated, captivated, equally astounded to see her. Her initial composed and perplexed expression swiftly transformed, giving way to anger simmering just beneath the surface. Their paths had indeed crossed before, and his presence brought back memories of events she had endeavored so ardently to forget.

Noticing her reaction, the esteemed Judge Sirius remarked,

"Today is your day in court. Please treat each other with respect and kindness. I understand that this encounter is far from pleasant, but it serves a purpose and carries significance that both of you must confront. You must speak the truth, the whole truth, and nothing but the truth. Lying or attempting to conceal the facts will be futile and only serve to needlessly prolong these proceedings. Fabrications will not alter the truth, which is unalterable and enduring, and will be revealed in due course. The figures seated behind you are witnesses to your testimonies. They possess ledgers that chronicle the histories of your karmic cycles. They may also stand here in representation of others who held significance during your lives, should the need arise. They have assumed the appearance of former loved ones to facilitate your arrival here in a manner acceptable to you. I apologize for the deception, but it was for the greater good of both parties."

Indeed, it had been a deception; her father had not been the one to bring her here. Isabella had been misled into believing she could be reunited with him, and although she wanted to feel sadness at that notion, she realized she no longer possessed the capacity for such emotions. She shifted uncomfortably in her chair, attempting to catch a glimpse behind her, realizing for the first time that the restraints that had held her in place had been slightly loosened. She believed every word spoken by the Judge and was certain that he already knew every detail of her life. There was no point in concealing anything, but that didn't mean this would be a pleasant experience. In fact, she was already convinced that it would be quite the opposite.

"DESTINY SHUFFLES THE CARDS; WE ARE JUST PLAYERS"

CHAPTER FOUR

THE LIFE STORIES

The trial's conclusion will soon bring about a complete transformation of the souls, liberating them from their physical identities and names, leaving behind only a pure pneuma. However, during the procedural initiation, Isabella's and Theo's names remain tightly intertwined with their souls.

"We shall commence," the Judge declared. "Does anyone wish to present their testimony first?"

Sensing Theo's hesitation to speak and the lingering silence, the Judge intervened. "Isabella, my dear child, perhaps you could begin by introducing yourself?"

Isabella murmured her name, followed by a prolonged pause of her own. The cloaked witness on her left somehow translated her feelings of panic and trepidation, as if capable of reading her thoughts and emotions churning deep within. It understood her, or rather, shared in her experience as if it were his own.

"Leave your concerns behind, Isabella," the Judge reassured. "Gaze upon the mystical pond, draw closer, immerse yourself in it. It shall revive your memories if you are uncertain. Simply ask, and it shall be revealed. Recollect a day when joy filled your heart, even if only for a fleeting moment, and relive it."

Released from her chair and driven by instinct, Isabella shuffled towards the edge of the pool and whispered softly, "Show me the day I won the prize for my art."

It had been an unforgettable moment for Isabella. Winning the prize during her final year in college had changed her life forever, though perhaps it could have been even more. And now she was reliving that day...

Suddenly, she found herself standing before a podium, her speech laid out before her in bold print. However, Isabella couldn't shake off the uneasiness brought on by the heavy silence of the crowded sports gym. She couldn't discern the hundreds of eyes fixed upon her, but she heard their anticipated whispers amidst the hush. Taking a calming breath, she attempted to read the first sentence of her speech, but her vision blurred as tears welled up in the corners of her eyes. Her entire school life condensed into that one day, encapsulated in a single piece of paper after nights of diligent work. Yet she couldn't articulate the words; tears overcame them, expressing her hope and joy for what lay ahead.

As the memory began to fade, the fog of her mind enshrouding that glorious day, Isabella decisively took a step into the water. It enveloped her skin in a refreshing, tingling embrace, and at her core, she sensed the water dispelling the fog like rhythmic waves, revealing forgotten details of the gymnasium. Craving more, she ventured further, aware that the pool could be an endless abyss that might sweep her away. However, she trusted the water, feeling its reassuring buoyancy keeping her afloat. She let herself fall backwards, knowing the water would support her. Serenely, the water responded, carrying her to the surface where she floated with half-closed eyes. It took her a moment to realize that she didn't feel wet in the slightest. All she felt was a profound sense of peace and warmth.

Like a tangled ball, the memory slowly unraveled, but it was only a matter of time before the joy of the award dissipated, giving way to a gloomy despair that gradually overshadowed Isabella's mood. The Judge was compelled to intervene, stepping into her thoughts to rouse her from the melancholy. "Isabella, my daughter," he said gently. "Focus."

Moving away from the memory of winning the award, Isabella recollected the moment when her husband, Eaton, had proposed to her. The occasion had been shared with her closest circle of friends, in one of her beloved venues. Comfort and happiness washed over her as she beheld the genuine smiles of her old friends, all brimming with laughter. Isabella now found herself standing in the soft glow of an upscale restaurant, where surfaces glistened, and ornate decorations added a touch of sophistication. Casting her gaze around the establishment, she suddenly felt butterflies in her stomach as the memory of what was about to unfold resurfaced, despite its unexpectedness at the time.

Her heartbeat quickened as Eaton rose from his seat and tentatively made his way towards her, a smile playing on his face. All her friends were focused on their every move, and only then did she realize that they must have been aware of what was about to transpire, even though she hadn't been. He lowered himself onto one knee and, with words he had undoubtedly rehearsed extensively, asked if she would consent to be his wife.

She hastened to respond before her emotions overwhelmed her completely. Without a moment's hesitation, she replied with confidence, "Yes!" Unable to contain herself, she was overcome with tears of joy and happiness, embracing him tightly.

Eaton 's own life story was fraught with intricate twists. Although he had grown up to become a renowned and highly accomplished businessperson, his youth had been marred by poverty and hardships. There had been numerous occasions when he had little to eat, and a stable roof over his head was far from guaranteed. Nevertheless, he managed to persevere and eventually flourish.

The perpetual scarcity of resources compelled him to abandon his education in order to earn a living. Despite being underage, he somehow secured a position in the kitchen of a cruise ship. Attaining the job had not been easy and involved obtaining a passport from a friend who bore a resemblance to him and was a few years older. This opportunity represented Eaton 's chance to escape the place he had grown up in and the life he had led. He was determined never to look back, and this was his breakthrough.

Constantly overworked, mistreated, and subjected to bullying by his superiors, Eaton struggled to find his footing. However, he kept his head down, toiled diligently, and absorbed as much knowledge as he could. As time passed, younger individuals joined the staff, some even younger than him, and he was no longer the target of abuse. He never felt remorseful that others were enduring hardships similar to those he had faced, for he had already served his time in that position; now it was someone else's turn.

The challenges he encountered compelled him to erect an impenetrable shield around himself. He shunned displays of emotions and severed ties with his family to avoid being reminded of the past he had labored so hard to forget. Work became his sole refuge from the haunting memories, becoming the focal point of his existence. One of the chefs noticed his eagerness to learn and his willingness to undertake any task to enhance his skills.

It was because he never had enough to eat while growing up, but his passion for food grew as he experienced new tastes and flavours. He wanted to learn everything he could about different foods. On his rare days off (when the ship was in port), he didn't spend time at pubs, casinos, or strip clubs like other crew members.

Instead, he explored local markets, savored street food, observed how it was prepared, and asked questions. He was always curious and eager to learn. Eventually, all that knowledge came in handy and helped him build his business.

As Eaton grew older, he established a hospitality empire, starting with his own street food stall inspired by the places he had visited. Over time, that single stall expanded into a chain of restaurants in city centers. Once these restaurants were running smoothly with minimal daily involvement from him, he delved into a partnership to acquire his first hotel. From there, he never looked back.

He first encountered Isabella at a hotel opening party and immediately sensed something special about her. She radiated confidence, strength, and femininity, despite being ten years his junior. She offered something that may have been lacking in his own youth.

Isabella's features set her apart from other women, arousing his curiosity. In his eyes, she appeared confident and self-assured, or at least that's what he had conveyed to her. All she knew about his past came from his own accounts; they were not her memories, but his. She had never known him before he became a successful hotel owner, and for the first time, she wondered if his stories were entirely true or if he had edited them to present himself in a certain light. This possibility had never crossed her mind before, and now she realized that she might never discover the truth. All she had ever known was the successful man.

They moved in circles that occasionally intersected, allowing their friendship to flourish, but their affair was initially kept a secret, to the point where no one could have suspected it.

Isabella was captivated by Eaton 's modesty and sincerity. Despite his success, he displayed no arrogance, unlike her narcissistic ex, Theo, who had drained her of life and left her feeling empty. Rebuilding her confidence had been a challenging journey, but she had finally reached a point where she felt she could trust a man again.

Isabella often found herself drawing comparisons between her lovers and her father, despite barely knowing him. She assumed this was a subconscious habit born out of longing and love. He had come and gone from her life, never staying long enough for her to truly know him, yet those fleeting moments remained vivid in her memory. Unconsciously, she searched for traces of him in every man who entered her life.

Eaton and Theo were no exceptions. She frequently compared them to her imagined version of her father and what she believed he would approve of. Theo reminded her of how she envisioned her father in his youth - audacious and brimming with self-confidence - while Eaton represented a more mature iteration of him.

It is not uncommon for children to develop feelings for individuals who resemble their parents in appearance or attitude, but Isabella's feelings towards her father were complex. She simultaneously loved and hated him, and the intensity of these conflicting emotions was equally astonishing. She loved him for the time he had spent with her and the hope that he would always remain, but she resented him for leaving, for not maintaining contact when a phone call or a letter would have been better than no communication at all. At times, he loved her unconditionally, but at others, he appeared to be indifferent.

Then she remembered what it was like when she was young and her father was living with them, but all she could recall was the constant fighting between her parents. They had never shown her enough love and affection during that time; they were too absorbed in their own problems to pay her sufficient attention.

Witnessing such violent arguments and traumatic events at home had led her to learn to tolerate abuse and suppress her natural reactions to assault. It was the only life she had known, and she had somehow thought it was normal. Now, all she could think of was the sound of slaps, crashing crockery, cries of pain and anger, and the endless slamming of doors.

Then the Judge's whispering voice broke through her memories. "Isabella, come back, be with us."

Unexpectedly, Isabella found herself no longer floating in the strange pool, but instead seated in her chair in the courtroom. It took a moment to recover from her memories, but even then, there was an echo of them that remained.

Theo had witnessed everything that had happened to Isabella, although she had not been aware at first that their memories were being shared. Her innermost thoughts and emotions had been laid bare without any masking. "Please, my child, feel free to talk to us through the memories if you wish."

Out of compassion and pity for his creations, the Judge kindly requested, "Water to the hall, please." The sound of rain came instantly; both souls looked up but there was no downpouring, only several rivulets that streamed down from above, crystal clear water that touched the floor and quickly spread to cover it. The water serenaded the vast room with a hallowed melody, not so much a sound that could be perceived by hearing, but a resonance in spirit. The water reached Isabella's feet, and as soon as it touched her, it diffused into her, rushing up to her core in a powerful surge. Its flow was a flux of coolness that wrapped around Isabella's Pneuma, completely overwhelming her angst and pain to leave behind a calm. The droplets reconvened into small streams and receded into the silvery pool. This event had a calming effect on the troubled and unsettled minds of the souls.

As the tense atmosphere in the room dissipated after Isabella's testimony, the Judge observed the changes the souls were going through. Satisfied with the outcome, he said to Theo, "Now, it is your turn to speak, Theo. Please remember to be sincere and honest; there is no room for deception in this place. Please introduce yourself."

Theo replied with confidence, "Yes, I understand. I am Theo Thomas. I passed away today due to a sudden heart attack, which brought me here."

"My son, can you tell us what caused your heart attack?" the Judge inquired. "It is important for us to understand."

Theo hesitated, not wanting to reveal the truth, but the Judge's warning about lying echoed in his mind. The court master sensed Theo's internal conflict and appealed to him in a peaceful yet firm manner. "Do not succumb to weaknesses, Theo. Be true to yourself."

Theo felt confused and embarrassed, as the words disarmed him completely. For the first time in his life, he was angry at himself instead of blaming others.

When a person with narcissistic tendencies is caught in a lie, instead of accepting it, they may manipulate the person in front of them to make them believe that the accusation is slanderous. If the person does not accept this, the issue may escalate, and sometimes the victim may deceive themselves due to their unhealthy and enthusiastic attachment. In such cases, love is truly blind.

Theo realized that resorting to lying would not yield the desired result, and although he was willing to tell the Judge what he needed to hear, he did not want to reveal his story in front of Isabella. He thought of asking the Judge directly for a private audience as there were just some aspects of his life that he was unwilling to be honest about, like the story of his failure, devastating downfall, and humiliation; this was not something he wanted to discuss in front of anyone else. Theo appealed to the court with an arrogant tone, saying, "I would like to request a private session. Matters of this intimate nature should not be shared with others. Forcing me to publicly reveal my personal affairs would undoubtedly violate my human rights."

The Judge's smoldering gaze did not flinch, but Theo felt the atmosphere shift in the room in response to his insolence. The witnesses of both souls clamoured—they showed no expressions but their aura-imposed disdain.

"Everyone is equal here, and all matters are treated equally. There are no exceptions. The only right you have, Theo, is to request equality if you feel you are not being treated fairly. I am here to ensure that fairness is provided to you without bias, but I must ask you to answer my questions. You have nothing to lose by giving your testimony in front of Isabella, and she has nothing to gain. None of it will be of any use to either of you when you leave this place."

Defeated, Theo's shoulders slumped as he replied, "Very well. I was betrayed by my wife. It turns out that she was cheating on me with my business partner. These individuals, whom I trusted the most, betrayed me. They may not have wielded a physical knife, but they certainly caused me great harm." Isabella's satisfaction at Theo's response unintentionally showed on her face as she smiled, seemingly happy that his life had ended unhappily. The consequence came like whiplash! She froze as intense heat burned inside her, but it was gone even before she could express discomfort. She removed the triumphant look from her face and felt a little ashamed of being caught, but not for the way she had felt.

She looked at the judge and realized that everyone's focus had shifted to her; even Theo stared intently. She had forgotten that they were connected in thought and memory! Sensing the anticipation of her response, Isabella spoke up for what she had just felt.

"As there is no point in hiding anything, my honest answer is that I am glad life didn't let this venomous snake live unpunished. He caused me a great deal of pain, and it seems only fair that he should have suffered somewhat in the same way."

"Is that what really makes you satisfied?" the Judge asked. "Or is there more to it than that?"

Isabella felt slightly embarrassed. "My high spirits can be explained by witnessing karma taking place. I am happy to learn that he has received the treatment he deserved. To see him finally caught has strengthened my belief in justice. This sack of arrogance and narcissism broke my own life."

"During our relationship, he mistreated me and manipulated my feelings. He blamed me for any of his wrongdoings, or anything that did not go the way he expected it to. He was exceptionally talented at finding ways of making me feel guilty for everything he did wrong. He always claimed that my words, trivial actions, gestures, or even appearance triggered the tricky situations which annoyed him. He justified his constant cheating on me, as well as his stealing and mistreatment, by blaming the way I treated him. Please believe me, he is a toxic man who would make a fool of anyone. But surely, he cannot fool you. You must have seen everything."

The Judge listened carefully and patiently. "Isabella, I must remind you to be respectful no matter what grievances you may hold against Theo! You must bear all in this grand courtroom. Tell us, tell us exactly how you feel about Theo."

Isabella's eyes filled with hate. "I am exceptionally angry with him. He is unfair, a charlatan, and in my eyes, his soul is worth nothing."

"Objection!" Theo couldn't help himself this time. "My soul was full of happiness because I wasn't an imposter or a liar like you, Isabella. I tried to make everyone happy, and I did not throw a tantrum every time your friends and allies made fun of me. I tolerated their mockery, their aggression, and their pathetic attempts to ridicule me. At times I felt they were doing it simply for their own amusement, but still, I didn't rise to it."

Isabella, stricken by the unfairness of this statement, crossed her arms and retorted, "So now a professional liar is claiming that I was caught lying? I was never any good at lying. That is why your accusations don't make any sense. You're disgusting. I only started realizing this more after you broke up with me. I just wish I had realized it sooner and taken matters into my own hands. I should have broken up with you first. I should have turned my back on you and walked away while I still had some self-respect."

Both of them lost control of their tempers, hurling insults at each other as they released pent-up feelings that had been simmering for so long. Their anger and bitterness escalated into an uncontrollable rage; they shouted at each other, determined to voice what had been buried deep in their hearts for too long, but neither of them listened to the other.

The Judge, aggrieved by their reaction, interrupted the clamor. “Order! I demand order in this courtroom!” Each word boomed with an ear-splitting clap of thunder! The foundations of the room shook, and the quake webbed fissures across the columns and floors.

The great Judge Sirius was patient and merciful, but dishonesty and disrespect invited his fury. Outbursts like this were rare, though not completely unprecedented, and almost always occurred when two souls were judged together. But it had been some time since he had last dealt with such a situation.

Both souls were silent, frozen in fear, gaping at the consequence of the Judge’s wrath.

“I demand your understanding and respect towards each other,” the Judge demanded. “The mutual disdain I observe here is beyond tolerance. Not a single living being should be subjected to such vile language. Do not let anger take over and speak for you. Your bantering is difficult to bear. This court has not been convened for you to simply insult each other. You had more than enough time to waste doing that on Earth. Now, listen to me carefully. This encounter is to give you the opportunity to find peace and the chance to forgive yourselves and each other. Do not waste it. Any further attempts to disobey will be met with my fury. It is not my wish for you to sequester in your anger or pain, neither is it my desire to chastise your outburst, but it is my duty to see that your unruliness is curbed. To that effect, this is your judgment day, and its proceedings must be forthright and judicious. This requires your utmost cordiality and amicability. You must tell the truth, but it has to be articulated with genuine repentance and without prejudice. Please be more respectful and loving. You are no longer a living person in the world, and it would do you well to leave all that negativity behind."

Isabella and Theo took the warning with a sense of fear, both realizing that the Judge likely had the power to destroy everything in an instant if they upset him. The lights in the room had started to blink and flicker since their argument, and Theo instantly connected this phenomenon of fluctuations in the intensity of the light to the aura of energy that surrounded the Judge; the presence of the Judge seemed to be the only thing illuminating everything. These fluctuations were caused by his conflict with Isabella. Drawing this conclusion, Theo and Isabella held their peace, ushering back perfect silence in the grand courtroom. A moment passed before the intensity of the aura around the great Judge began to increase, re-establishing illumination to the farthest parts of the courtroom.

The Judge, satisfied, resumed the conversation. "Theo, please tell us about your family and your childhood."

"I wouldn't describe my childhood as particularly happy," Theo began, this time without hesitation. "Although I believe my parents loved each other, at least at first, they both craved their own freedom. I was their only child, but attention and affection were only given to me in moderation. I was a bright student, but my parents never showed much interest in my success, and they did not guide me in life. Their desire for freedom often led to arguments, and I suspect that many of their fights were about me and the responsibility I placed on them. Most of their arguments ended with my father leaving and not returning for months at a time.

"Even when he was living away from our home, he would still occasionally pick me up from school and take me out for dinner or some other activity. He tried to maintain some sort of bond between us, I suppose, but now I wonder whether he did it out of love or some perceived duty, although that never crossed my mind at the time. I thought he did it because he wanted to spend time with me, because he loved me, even if he didn't always show it."

"My mother would verbally abuse and emasculate him, and I hated it. Seeing this kind of behavior from the woman who was supposed to create a peaceful and loving home shaped my perception of women. I vowed that I would never let any future wife of mine show disrespect towards me like my mother did to my father. She would have to speak to me kindly and respectfully, and any attempts to rebel against this would be met with force. It was the only way."

"I wanted my wife to be perfect, humble, and obedient, to never contradict me. I wanted her to be a complete contrast to the woman who raised me. I wanted her to fully accept me, everything I said and did, without objection, without any conditions. Adoration and worship, which is what I sought in a woman. Was that really too much to ask for?"

The Judge waited for Theo to finish, ignoring Isabella's gasp of surprise and disbelief, expressions she tried to stifle. It was evident that she couldn't quite believe what she was hearing.

"What you desired, my son, was an unequal bond," the Judge said. "The union you were seeking would be no different from what your parents had, where you would take the dominating role, the role your mother used to play. You wanted to manipulate, oppress, and enslave someone who loved you. God does not create anyone to be perfect on purpose. You tried to make yourself God, but you are not God, and you cannot make anyone treat you like Him. What you wanted, Theo, is slavery, and you should always beware of slaves. They can revolt."

"The outcome of an encounter between two souls can result in either mutual evolution or harm. The karmic debt soars in the aftermath of harmful contact, which has to be repaid eventually. Karma transcends lifetimes until it is balanced out. You need to understand and master your karmic lesson and pay the debt. This can only be achieved by seeking truth and love."

"Giving love and speaking the truth will determine the end of your karmic cycle. It is only complete if you address the debts, raise awareness around it, and treat others respectfully. God repeatedly exposes you to challenges to show that there is a better way to solve these challenges, but you must find the solution yourself. He wants you to learn, to understand, and evolve. You can either cultivate awareness, to understand and address your karma, or you can keep spinning karmic cycles. The choice is yours, and only yours."

"I was unable to find the love I was looking for in anyone," Theo answered.

"To find true love, Theo, you must first learn to love yourself. How can anyone give love if this feeling is yet to be understood and fully realized? You wanted someone to adore you just to satisfy your ego, while you gave nothing in return. Love is a cruel feeling that does not tolerate selfishness."

Theo tried to explain himself, without fully understanding what he was trying to say. "I saw no love while I lived on Earth, not even when I was a child looking for it in my family. And it escaped me when I tried to find it in women too."

"I remember after another fight with my dad, my mother packed her things and left home; it was the only time I remembered her being the one to leave. She walked out without looking at me, even though I begged her to stay. I was just seven years old. I remember grabbing hold of her skirt as tightly as I could to try to stop her, but she just kicked me, pulled her skirt close to her, and stepped over me as if I were no more than rubbish in the street. The pain I felt in that moment was not physical, I swear I could have endured a thousand kicks if it would have made her stay, but she stepped over me as if I was an obstruction. As if I was just a nuisance and not her son. She didn't come back for months, and in all that time, I didn't see her once, never knowing if she would ever come back. But every morning I woke up, hoping that would be the day she returned."

"Although I had a nanny, I felt abandoned, and I wanted my mother back. The day she left, and for many more after that, I cried in my room for hours until I fell asleep. My mother had abandoned me, and that is why I hated her. I promised myself that I would not let any woman leave me again. I was not going to be abandoned again, so I decided to always be the one to end a relationship. I learned at a very young age not to trust anyone, especially women."

Isabella found herself feeling confused, even a little sorry for him. This was the first time she had heard Theo talk about his feelings and his reasons for being the way he was. Before this, she had never found any justification for his behavior, but now, all the dots had been connected in her mind, and so much made sense. She felt nothing but pity for him; the hate and loathing that had been there had slowly disappeared.

She just saw a seven-year-old boy begging his mother not to abandon him.

Theo, typically reserved in his emotions, felt a sense of relief after sharing the burden he had carried on his shoulders for so many years. A weight had been lifted that he had not even been aware of, which had been weighing him down.

Judge Sirius was already aware of their struggles, secrets, and thoughts, but the purpose of the hearing was for the souls to learn and understand them too. Without understanding, they could not change, and without change, the Karmic debt could never be paid. Theo and Isabella needed to go through this conversation to resolve their resentment and find balance. What was said during this procedure wouldn't change anything, but it might heal the wounds and bring peace of mind. However, understanding could only be achieved by telling the truth.

Honesty loses its effect when unraveled too late or at an unsuitable moment. Theo and Isabella were telling the truth because the Judge already knew everything to the smallest detail and was able to point out if they were failing to tell the truth. They had no real choice.

Isabella tentatively tried to attract the Judge's attention. She felt that the balance had not yet been reached, and she had more to say, yet she felt unwilling to break the silence that followed Theo's revelation.

"Isabella, I see there is another story you want to tell us," The Judge said after allowing a moment for the implications of Theo's testimony to be considered, not only by Isabella but also by Theo himself. This was the first time he had revealed such intimate details of his past, and he needed a moment to come to terms with this as much as Isabella did.

Isabella humbly smiled at the omniscient Judge. "Actually, I was a loving person and always wanted this feeling to be mutual. Who wouldn't want that? Is that too much to ask of any relationship? As I grew older, I realized that the only love I really needed to look for was the love of the creator. Without that, there is nothing."

"The soul being judged along with me today has left scars on many lives. By sharing in his memories, I have witnessed and experienced the way he treated a loving woman. Though I am proud of the love I gave, I feel humiliated at the same time. Instead of love, he showed me pain, and that cannot be right. We were both in our twenties when we first met. I saw him playing the guitar on the street and fell in love with him instantly.

My heartbeat faster, and I felt flushed, too shy to say anything to him. All I managed was a small smile."

The Judge stopped her before she could tell her story. "It would be better if we could all see your memories of the time you spent with Theo, particularly your early meetings."

Isabella waited for a moment before replying. She knew that the Judge wanted her to return to the pool, and even though this time she knew what would happen, she was happy to do as he requested. Her fear had somewhat subsided, and the pool seemed less frightening than it was before. This was not about her; it was about Theo.

“SADNESS IS
WHEN THE
LAST LEAF FALLS
FROM THE TREE
IN AUTUMN”

CHAPTER FIVE

FIRST MEETING

It was lunchtime on a sunny day, and shoppers were taking advantage of the fine weather. The granite pavements and boulevard lanes drew attention to street art, restaurants, and offices. The bustling flow of people surged in opposite directions; some hurried into the underground, and others lingered at bus stops or pedestrian crossings. A few others sought refuge in the shade of trees along the boulevard lanes, casually seated on benches and engrossed in books. There was a shared ambiance as each person purposefully immersed themselves in the monotony of their day. While some sat to soak in the atmosphere of that sunny afternoon, others hopped from store to store, pausing now and then to admire window displays. Amidst this eclectic mix, a distinct melody resonated somewhere, and the artist had already gathered a small, dynamic audience. His fans listened in silent admiration as he plucked chords to a romantic song, entwining his audience with his mastery and captivating their hearts with his melodious tenor. Isabella did not notice it initially amidst the chatter of her friends. She had slipped away momentarily to grab a sandwich and coffee for lunch, but she was not in any great hurry.

The young man was performing in front of a closed shop, not obstructing the pedestrian flow, but in a location where many passersby would encounter him. Every time a coin was dropped into his open guitar case, he swiftly expressed his gratitude without breaking the rhythm of the song he was singing. Across the street, there was an available table on the café terrace, and she seized the impromptu opportunity to claim it. There was something about his voice that made her want to listen a little longer, and today, she could spare the time.

Shoppers and office workers came and went, with some adding a few coins to his collection, while others simply walked by. Even those who paused to listen for a while didn't all contribute. There was a tinge of sadness in that, but it didn't seem to disturb him. And as soon as someone walked away, someone else stepped in to take their place. He simply continued playing, most of the time lost in the melody.

Isabella knew most of the songs he played. She had heard some of them on the radio when she was a child, although the young man appeared to be about the same age as her. Yet, a few of the songs were unfamiliar to her. She found herself wondering if they were simply lesser-known songs or if they were his own compositions. He was evidently a skilled musician; she was captivated by the dexterity of his hands as they moved effortlessly over the guitar strings. But truthfully, it was his smile rather than his voice or his skill that had her enthralled.

After staying there longer than she had intended, she stepped inside to settle her bill. When she emerged, clutching a couple of coins to drop into his case, she discovered that the singer had already packed up and left. Isabella couldn't help but feel a little deflated. She had worked up the courage to cross the road, to contribute to his collection, and exchange a smile. She might not have thought beyond that, but it had been a start, and now she had missed the opportunity. She tucked the coins into her jacket pocket with a tinge of disappointment, gave one last glance at the empty doorway, and headed back.

Over the next couple of days, Isabella passed by the same café at least once daily, half hoping to see him in the same spot, but there was no sign of him. He must have moved on to another location, hoping for a few more coins to come his way. On the third day, he was back in his usual spot when she walked past, but this time she was in a hurry and couldn't spare more than a couple of minutes to listen.

As she stood and listened to his performance, she rummaged in her bag, searching for a contribution to add to his guitar case, but only found a couple of loose pennies. It would be an insult to drop them in the case. She closed her bag, slung the strap over her shoulder, and began to walk past him. He still gave her a smile. She had barely taken a dozen steps when she remembered the pound coins, she had put in her jacket pocket. They were still there. She took a deep breath, turned on her heels, and retraced her steps. Just as she was about to drop the coins into the case, his song ended.

"Thank you," he said, giving her the widest smile. "You didn't have to come back."

"I wanted to," she said. "I had just forgotten that I had some change on me."

She explained to him how she had wanted to give him something a couple of days ago, but he had left before she had the chance.

"Sorry," he said. "It was getting quiet," he confirmed, indicating that he had gone elsewhere to try his luck.

"It can't be easy," she said, glancing down at the collection of coins in the guitar case. The copper coins at the bottom of her bag wouldn't have seemed out of place. There were a few other pound coins alongside the two she had dropped herself. It wasn't much.

"I'd buy you a coffee," he said, following her gaze. "But..."

Isabella laughed. "I'd buy you one," she said. "But I need to be somewhere. Will you be here tomorrow?"

He smiled again, and she felt herself blushing. "I can make sure I am," he said.

"In that case, I'll buy you a coffee then," Isabella said. "And if you're really lucky, I might even buy you a sandwich."

She didn't wait for his answer; she simply turned and walked away, surprised at her own bravado.

"See you then," he called after her. "My name's Theo."

She smiled but kept walking. He was going to have to wait until the following day to find hers.

The following day was a Saturday, and Isabella had plenty of free time, but she didn't want to arrive too early. She had hardly slept that night, and when she did, she dreamt about Theo singing to her, and more. Even when she was awake, he was all she could think about. It was ridiculous; all she knew about him was his name.

She got ready far too early, with at least an hour of spare time to kill. Trying to distract herself with frivolous things at her apartment, she finally succumbed to the pressure and went to see Theo. She walked half a mile to the shopping center where she had seen him, pausing at every shop window along the way to pass the time.

After spending a few more minutes looking in the window of a shop selling outdoor wear, she checked her watch and saw that it was almost twelve. Still earlier than the time they had agreed upon, but she hoped she wouldn't seem too eager, even if she was.

His guitar case seemed to have a few more coins than it did the day before, most likely because more people were out and about. He gave her a smile as she approached but didn't stop playing his song. It was one she knew, and she felt like singing along, but she refrained. Instead, she patiently waited until he finished before approaching him.

"Looks like you're having a better day," she said, glancing down.

"A little," he said. "But I'm not sure if I have enough to buy you lunch."

"My treat," Isabella said. "I offered, remember."

"Your very kind, but I still don't know your name. I can't accept such charity if I don't know your name."

"Isabella!" she replied, her cheeks blushing with flirtatious energy.

"Well then, Isabella. Where are we going?" He gathered the change from his case and placed his guitar in it. She hadn't even thought about him needing to bring it along, but it wasn't an issue. They could take it to the café across the road where she had seen him earlier in the week. As luck would have it, there was an available table outside when they crossed the road.

They talked about anything and everything, soon engaging in conversation like lovers, never running out of things to discuss. An hour passed, then two, before Isabella realized how much time had flown by.

"Oh no," she said, realizing that she had been preventing him from earning his living. "I'm so sorry, I've kept you talking for too long."

"Don't worry about it. It's been delightful."

"It has," Isabella said. "But you should get back over there."

He stooped and picked up his guitar case. "Thank you," he said. "Shall we do this again?"

She stood up as well, desiring to look him in the eyes rather than having to look up at him.

"I'd like that," she said. "I'd like that very much."

He leaned forward and kissed her on the cheek, catching her off guard. She blushed deeply as warmth rose in her chest along with the butterflies in her stomach. It was sweet and brought a slight blush to her face. He fished in his pocket for a slip of paper and gave it to her. "My number," he said. "Don't hesitate to use it."

She used it frequently enough, texting him a few times first, and barely able to wait until that evening before calling him. Late into the night, they continued their conversation...

Isabella opened her eyes to find herself back in her seat. She was certain that she must have entered the pool to share the memory, but she couldn't recall it. Theo was looking at her. She thought he seemed relieved. She wondered if she had revealed something he had forgotten, something he thought she might use against him.

"Thank you, my child," the Judge said. "It's good to see that in your eyes, the beginning of your relationship was innocent and that there was no indication that Theo had bad intentions."

"Why would she even think that?" Theo said, a little annoyed, shooting her an accusing glance.

"I didn't," Isabella said. "I never have. I fell in love with you, I honestly believed you loved me too. At least, I did at first."

"Please," the Judge insisted. "Try to remain calm and tell the court whatever it is you wish it to consider."

Isabella took a deep breath and began again, not returning to the pool this time. These were merely words she wanted to share.

"We started meeting more frequently. My career was just beginning, and occasionally, we discussed art and exchanged ideas for new paintings. He told me about his dreams of becoming famous and wealthy. Our chats covered various topics, and he displayed his obsession with money during almost every episode."

"I didn't think much of it initially. We both aspired for success; me with my painting, him with his music, and we both understood that money would come with it. For me, it meant security. It would provide me with the time to create paintings I truly wanted to make, rather than just for the sake of selling. But for Theo, it was different. It was as if money held greater importance to him than his music. It saddened me to hear how money mattered so much to him, but I never voiced my thoughts because I didn't want to bring him down. In a jesting manner, I used to say, 'Theo, I'll paint a portrait of you that I'm certain you won't like because it will reveal your true face and passion.'"

"Later in my career, I followed through with this idea. I am not entirely sure why, whether it was to immortalize my mistake or to caution others about the kind of person we can become. I can't say for certain. Nonetheless, I drew inspiration from him and created a painting I titled 'Blind Narcissist Frog.' It gained recognition from critics and brought me fame. It almost feels as though it was my destiny to make such a playful mockery. If you observe the painting, you'll see a young man with a frog-like face, devoid of arms, attempting to play a guitar. His heart is exposed outside his body, and his eyes are covered by the sun and the moon."

"At the start of our relationship, we got along splendidly. We comprehended each other without needing excessive communication, and we frequented the same café, engaging in endless conversations without growing weary. It felt as though nothing and no one else existed when I was with him. It didn't take long for us to progress from café conversations to inviting him into my home, my life, and my bed."

She paused for a moment, as if expecting the Judge to comment on morality, on the hastiness of their relationship. As if she believed some of it could be her fault. However, he remained silent, the lighting unchanged, and in that instant, the room fell into silence.

"I cared for him deeply," she continued, "I longed for him, even when he was merely in another room. At times, I felt as though God was punishing me by bestowing upon me such intense and overwhelming emotions. It consumed me entirely, and there were moments when he was all I could think about."

"But then, a peculiar thought entered my mind. The creator loves those who love, not those who worship. I am unsure where it came from—I may have heard or read it somewhere. I realized that this love I had for Theo was causing me more pain with each passing day. My family and friends attempted to warn me, stating that he wasn't a good match for me, that he didn't treat me well, and that I should end the relationship. Those words filled me with deep sorrow, and I began to resent them simply because they didn't love him. They failed to comprehend the bond we shared. Looking back on that time now, I see that they were right, and I should have heeded their advice instead of turning a blind eye."

He made me believe that my friends and family despised me, and that he was the only one in the entire world who truly loved me. He encouraged me to sever all ties with the people closest to me, and I found myself with absolutely no one left to confide in except him. Initially, it didn't seem to matter because we had each other, and that should have sufficed, but I was a complete wreck—heartbroken, wounded, and lonely. It was only after he left me that I realized this hadn't been true love."

"We vacated the flat that I adored, with a spare bedroom that I used as a studio and rented a small house together. It was terribly cramped and lacked space for my cherished studio. It wasn't at all what I had wanted, and I expressed my dissatisfaction at the time. We didn't have intense arguments about it, but we did bicker back and forth. In the end, it was his desire that prevailed. Everything was centered around what he wanted."

"My dream had been to excel in my career, purchase a nice house, and live happily with him. Regrettably, he shattered that dream. He constantly found reasons to break up with me, reasons why we shouldn't be together, yet I did everything in my power to please him so he wouldn't abandon me. I invested so much time and emotional energy just to keep him by my side. I was utterly blind to his manipulative tactics."

"Theo had a deep passion for music and dreamed of attaining fame, performing at one of the grand festivals for thousands of fans. I didn't require that level of adoration; I simply wanted a few people to appreciate my work. We hadn't been cohabiting for long when his friend Emma appeared. She owned a music company and offered him a job to advance his career. At the time, she was married and had three children, but initially, I didn't realize the romantic involvement between her and Theo."

"Even when I discovered that they were having an affair, I feigned ignorance because I wanted him to be happy. I thought he had found something I couldn't provide. Admitting it was painful, but at the same time, I was still content, I suppose."

"One day, I overheard him conversing with Emma on the phone about his plan to leave me for her. I cannot express how much it hurt; I couldn't hold back my tears. The following day, I gathered whatever remained of my self-respect and somehow managed not to confront him about his infidelity, but instead watched and waited. Although fully aware of his betrayal, I couldn't bring myself to act maliciously towards Theo because I still loved him deeply. What shattered me completely was the way he left me."

"I was prepared to calmly discuss his cheating and was even willing to forgive him, but he callously denied me that option. He departed without a 'sorry,' without a 'thank you,' not even the cliché 'we could remain friends.' He disregarded all the moments and memories, all the time we had spent together, and everything we had ever said to each other, simply texting 'Goodbye.' So, I was left with nothing but this emotionless and faceless 'Goodbye.'"

"As soon as I received that message, I rushed back home. All of his belongings were gone, along with a bottle of my favorite perfume, which he had given me for my birthday. The house, already dreary before, became unbearable. Its oppressive emptiness weighed me down. I lay motionless on the bedroom floor for two nights, hoping it was all just a nightmare—unfortunately, it wasn't."

"After two days, my colleagues noticed my absence and expressed concern for my wellbeing. They came to the house to check on me and found me lying on the floor and helped me to survive. I don't know what I would have done without them."

Theo was both ashamed and offended by this story and kept trying several times to interrupt Isabella and begging the Judge to make her stop. Nothing was allowed to stop her testimony. This had been as much for her benefit: a chance to fully express herself.

CHAPTER SIX

DECISION TIME

The room was becoming warm and stuffy despite its size. The energy released from the heated conversations had filled the hall with a presence so tangible that it felt like a cloak draped over the room. The souls were exhausted but filled with such relief that they had almost nothing else to talk about. The bad memories had been expelled from their bodies, and the wounds were ready to heal. The great Judge Sirius scanned the room.

"You are soul mates," he said. "Even if you choose to live separate lives, your energies are of similar frequencies, which is why your encounters are inevitable and your destinies alike. Think about the good moments you shared. There is no point in resonating anymore; find your ground state. You have so much to add to each other's existence. You shouldn't mirror each other's shortcomings because that will only cause more wounds."

After some thought, Isabella replied, "Yes, he inflicted countless wounds on me because of the trauma his mother made him live through. But I am not to blame for that. I was exposed to his misogyny and anger for actions and events I had no control over. I was innocent and had no responsibility for what made him hate women." When she said this, her shoulders dropped, and the tension between her shoulder blades disappeared. It was as if she had long been tethered to an anvil, but finally, that attachment snapped free. She hadn't realized it until now, but this burden had weighed on her for years.

"This woman was created powerful yet elegant," said the Judge. "What do you say, Theo? Would you like to reject her words in the face of justice?"

Theo responded softly and honestly, not in a tone of defensiveness but with a sigh of admittance and care, "I liked her too, but the fact is that she wasn't entirely honest with me. Her family didn't like me, and neither did her friends. They criticized and ridiculed me in order to break the bond between Isabella and me, but she decided not to listen to them and chose to stand by my side instead. She left everything behind. She refused her friends, her life, and herself. I liked her, and I didn't want her to abandon her true self. But she betrayed herself and walked away, just like my mother did. How does that make her a better woman then?"

"When she chose this path, there was no Isabella left, nothing that I liked. I recognize the power of her action to abandon everything for me, but I didn't ask for it. I didn't ask her to find absolute emptiness after she rejected her former life. I couldn't fill the void she created within herself, and neither could Isabella. After a while, her emptiness became uncomfortable, and I grew bored of it. I couldn't find my Isabella anymore. I disconnected, and it frightened and disappointed me. I had thought I could never get attached to anyone, and that made me sad. I suppose I was deeply and utterly lonely."

"The first time I fell in love was at school. However, somehow, I created an insurmountable distance between us, which broke the girl's heart. I cannot explain why, but apparently, this is how I am. In moments when relationships are expected to grow more intimate, I tend to withdraw. I am just afraid of being the one who gets hurt.

"The same applies to my inability to admit to mistakes and apologize because acknowledging failure shortens the distance between people, and again, when I feel it too close, I retreat. I couldn't overcome this dark aspect of myself, even with the ones I believed I truly loved. I suppose I am emotionally reserved and unable to express my feelings to anyone."

"Since I couldn't show affection or approach the person I liked, I expected them to come to me. However, that girl left me without a word. She just disappeared. It made me ill, and I suffered from severe depression. I searched for her, trying to find her face in everyone I saw. When I realized I wouldn't find her, my sorrow turned into anger. No one could leave me; only I could be the one to do that."

Judge Sirius interrupted Theo. "It's unfair, Theo, to torment yourself and others by lacking emotional intelligence and hiding your true feelings. Life is more stubborn and patient than you are, and you should know that. Even if you don't admit the mistakes you make, your conscience does. You feel its impact when you toss and turn in bed, unable to sleep."

"Then you face a new day, live your life, and try to forget about it. But once your head hits the pillow, your struggle resumes. You are awake again, haunted by your mistakes, and they won't let you sleep. Wherever you go, they are with you; you cannot erase them."

"You are fighting with yourself; you endlessly replay what you did. You still try to conceal your inner battle from everyone, but you cannot hide it from yourself. You become your own worst enemy."

Theo confessed, "I have suffered from this for years. I couldn't express myself. I wanted to tell my father so many things, but I couldn't. I wanted to tell him how much I loved him and admit that I made a huge mistake by leaving him alone during the hardest time of his life. I miss him; he was a good friend I could always talk to. After I lost him, my uncle took his place. I thought I could overcome grief more quickly by replacing the lost person with someone else. They said I resembled my uncle a lot, though I suspect they didn't mean that in a positive way, but we got along."

"My uncle abandoned his family due to his stubbornness and narcissism, though I'm not sure I realized that at the time. He slandered his wife and left without a word, leaving her and their two children behind. I acknowledge that such behavior is terrible and unfair, but I saw how comfortable he was with his decision to shirk his responsibilities. I missed my father deeply and wanted to talk to him one last time, but I couldn't. It was all because I knew I had messed up and broken his heart too."

"I was certainly in the wrong, but I couldn't admit it to my dad. Deep down inside, I knew my mistake, but I would always convince myself that what I had done was right. And so, I replaced my loved ones with others whom I treated the same way, partly to prove to myself that it was the right way to behave. At times, those who worked under me suffered from my unfair actions and stubbornness, and the more I acted in this manner, the more my ego inflated. The inability of people to confront me only reinforced my behavior. I believed that everything I did was right because it was comfortable for me and my ego."

"It was difficult to cope with the loss of my father. I missed him, I couldn't believe that he had left me, and I longed for him to return. I started noticing that every detail, every face, and even every house reminded me of him. The guilt I felt for what I had done to him, and the inability to rectify it, was suffocating. I made the decision to go abroad and start afresh, promising myself to lead a better life. I simply wanted to forget everything that had transpired and give myself a new beginning."

"I packed up all my belongings and relocated to Los Angeles with the hope of building a new life. I secured a job in a boutique hotel managed by my father's friend. Unfortunately, this phase of my life mirrored the past. One mistake followed another once again. I fell in love with Lucia, my boss's wife. I was well aware that she was off-limits, but I couldn't control myself, especially knowing that she harbored feelings for me too. Despite my boss's mistreatment and the consistent delay in paying my salary, I stayed there for four years simply because I loved his wife."

"It was the forbidden aspect, perhaps the thrill of danger, which kept our relationship alive. However, Lucia didn't share my excitement and told me to go back to where I had come from. I hesitated before deciding to leave, fearing that she might confess our affair to her husband. It was a hasty decision, but I returned to London. Once again, I suppressed my feelings. I didn't even allow them to surface when I realized that I would never see her again."

"When I returned to London, I had very little, just a bag of clothes and enough cash to buy a cheap guitar and cover a month's rent for a bedsit. I started busking and playing music to earn enough money for daily sustenance and to save for the next month's rent.

Some days, I couldn't even earn enough to accomplish that. It was during this period that I met Isabella."

"I wish I had never met you," Isabella sadly remarked, a slight frown etched on her lovely face. "It was only after you left me that I understood your manipulative motives. I had suspected that you needed me to provide you with a roof over your head, but that didn't bother me. I was helping you pursue your dream. However, you attempted to devalue and break me, to mold me into someone who would unquestioningly do everything you desired. Your toxic arguments drained my energy, and there were moments when I felt so exhausted that I could no longer resist the nonsensical ideas you preached. I allowed them to take root in my mind and deplete all my resources."

"Then you left me, and the emptiness of losing you engulfed me like a black hole. And indeed, I perished and was reborn, emerging from the wreckage of my former self. I learned how to live without you, how to cease longing for your presence, and how to rekindle my self-appreciation."

"Gradually, I expelled your presence from my surroundings, my thoughts, and my life. I managed to replenish my energy, and you became a distant memory.

Nothing reminded me of you; there were no remaining connections between us. I eradicated you from my life. A loving woman can make a man stronger when he treats her with respect and attentiveness, but when she is subjected to abuse and mistreatment, she forfeits her power and strength."

The Judge interjected, "Love is a mysterious sentiment. Our creator fashioned men and women and held a profound love for them, even when his creations made mistakes. The creator always remembers his children and loves them unconditionally. He offers support when they encounter difficulties, although people often disregard this support because they fail to recognize it for what it truly is."

"At times, the creator attempts to reach your soul through other individuals or events in your life. He communicates with you, even if you are unable to hear him. If you were to listen to your heart and follow the signs it presents, you would comprehend his message."

Isabella endeavored to heed her heart. "Forgive me but does the creator have love for men or women?" she inquired.

"He created men and women to complement one another and certainly not to discriminate based on gender," Judge Sirius replied. "Everything on Earth that the creator has ever made combines attributes from different genders. When you contemplate the beauty and gentleness of blossoming flowers and trees, you might perceive it as portraying femininity, whereas if you acknowledge the power and strength of lightning and thunder in the sky, you will undoubtedly associate it with masculinity."

"A fully functioning and balanced system can only be achieved when all genders are involved. A child can grow and develop properly only when they feel affection and protection from both parents and our creator. The creator is always connected with you, whether you desire it or not. His light will guide you through the darkness if you seek help, but he allows you to find your own way if you don't reach out to him. He is constantly aware of you, wherever you may be, as a part of your life resides within him."

Theo listened silently to the Judge and then asked, "Why do we all die? If he loves us, why does the creator allow children to endure the pain of losing a parent or people to mourn the loss of loved ones? And where do we go after life is over? We are all sinners, so are we all destined to burn in hell?"

"You are not an attentive listener, Theo, are you? This question brings us back to the conversation about karma and karmic debt. When a person dies without fulfilling their karmic debts, they enter another cycle of reincarnation to repay what is owed. If the lesson is not learned during their lifetime, their spiritual journey remains incomplete. The individual must confront their own debt."

"As for your question, Theo, everyone's concept of heaven and hell is different. What one person may fear, another may dream of. However, God is omniscient and knows your fears, allowing the devil to see them as well. He presents you with tests and challenges to awaken your darkest energy and tempt you to commit sin. One wrong decision or a failed test, and you move closer to your own personal hell. God provides numerous opportunities to change your path and make the right choices. He watches as you shape your destiny, constantly seeking to improve it. Ultimately, it is your decision which path you choose: the one leading to hell or the one leading to heaven. Fire has its positive and negative aspects. It is a simplistic view to think of hell merely as a place of eternal fire."

Judge Sirius gestured towards the pool, and an image appeared on its surface. It depicted two souls who were once lovers but had separated in their past lives. Witnessing the story of their previous encounter, Isabella felt compelled to share another memory of Theo, prompting the Judge to say, "Isabella, my daughter, please share what is on your mind."

Isabella, still gazing at the pool, spoke, "After our breakup, I moved into a friend's house, one of the few I still had even though I hadn't treated her as well as I should have, because everything in the house we had shared with Theo was so painful, reminding me of losing him. However, I later discovered that he had rented the same house again. I felt the need to go there to see him once more, to find closure."

"I knocked on the door, and Theo opened it. He appeared surprised to see me and pretended as if nothing had ever happened between us. He asked if I needed anything. I felt strange and disconnected from him. I told him that I had forgotten some of my belongings and had come to retrieve them. In reality, I had only gone there to see him, and he must have known that too. There was nothing of mine left in that house. I had checked every drawer and cupboard, ensuring that I would never need to return."

"I was wearing a green dress, which I later gave away because I couldn't bear to wear it anymore. It reminded me of that final meeting and seemed to carry Theo's negative energy whenever I even glanced at it. It served as a constant reminder of him and everything he had put me through. The moment I stepped into the house, I sensed negative energy throughout the space and almost immediately felt ill. I couldn't stay there for another moment. I stepped back outside, closed the door, and thought about how much I wished he would come after me, but he didn't. He didn't even open the door to watch me leave."

"I had dreamt of him embracing me and begging me to stay. Well, my dream didn't come true. Instead, it only confirmed that he didn't care, and I suspect he never did. I cried that night, pleading with the creator and questioning why I deserved such treatment. Almost immediately after that night, I was able to completely forget about him."

Theo also remembered that day. "I cried when you left that day too, Isabella. I wanted to chase after you and prevent you from leaving, but something held me back. I don't know what it was. Your appearance ignited a conflict within me, and I couldn't muster the strength to overcome my ego. It was only later that I realized I had met the right person at the wrong time."

Judge Sirius inquired, "Isabella, how did your experience with Eaton compare to your time with Theo? Were you content with him?"

"When I met Eaton," Isabella replied, "it wasn't love at first sight. I even had the impression that he didn't particularly like me. Breaking up with Theo left a profound resentment in my heart, and I suppose I had nearly lost faith in love. My heart was in anguish, and I struggled to create anything that interested anyone. My early success had evaporated, and I began to believe that I would never be able to make a living solely from my art. The savings I had managed to accumulate were slowly dwindling as I tapped into them to support my living expenses. I needed to find a job, even if it didn't involve art."

"I focused on trying to secure employment, but I faced rejection from every potential employer I applied to. This situation persisted, and I gradually sank into depression. Somehow, I managed to obtain a job at the library near my home. At the same time, I continued to draw pictures and attempted to sell them on the street where other artists gathered. The regular income from the library allowed me to at least cover my rent and sell a few pieces of art provided for some luxuries, like food. I prayed to God for assistance, but then I was informed that the library had to close. I had rebelled against God, yet he had answered my prayer."

Maybe if I hadn't heard that the library was closing and hadn't gone to the pub that day, I would never have met Vicky. Vicky played a significant role in recognizing my paintings. She admired my ambition and the style of my artwork. She owned a gallery, and initially, she hired me as a sales assistant. Later on, she even exhibited some of my paintings. Everything was going well, and I could solely focus on my work. My life became more organized, and my sleep improved. I regained my energy, and I suppose I grew closer to God."

Judge Sirius remarked, "God always creates opportunities to offer assistance. It is up to the individual to perceive the right message. He observes you in different situations and leaves the choice to you. Your destiny rests in your own hands. What may appear as a coincidence is actually God's intervention because you prayed to Him for help in making your choice."

"Yes," Isabella confirmed. "I followed every sign whispered in my ear as if good things were awaiting me.

Some time passed, and every painting I created started to attract attention. I used to depict beings that combined aspects of animals and humans. I had developed my own style and felt excited about it all over again. It began capturing the media's attention, and the sudden progress in my career made me feel even stronger. God cleared my path and encouraged me, saying, 'Come on, Isabella, strive for success.' I recognized the power within me, and my soul was advancing towards enlightenment. While my professional life was on track, my love life was nonexistent. It seemed impossible for me to love or fall in love with anyone again. I was highly sensitive and experienced every emotion intensely. I constantly reminded myself that love was not bound by worldly limitations."

"My circle of friends was nearly nonexistent as well. Old acquaintances had drifted away, and in truth, I had pushed some of them away. I had only one close girlfriend, Madeline, who offered me a place to stay when I left the house I had shared with Theo. She always listened to me and provided motivation. She is now married and has a daughter, and I had moved out of her spare room and into a new apartment. Later, rumors began to circulate that I was having an affair with her.

Madeline's husband was extremely unhappy with this situation and wanted her to sever ties with me."

"Frankly, I was upset about this situation too because I didn't want to lose our friendship. Initially, our relationship was purely platonic, but it gradually evolved into something much deeper. I didn't realize what these feelings were. They were new to me; unlike anything I had experienced before with another woman. It was a profound sense of love. I believed that true love transcended gender differences, existing solely within the realm of the soul.""I sought God in every gaze that met mine, in every meaningful conversation, and in the beauty of my childhood dreams. Somehow, I had discovered something wonderful in Madeline."

CHAPTER SEVEN

AZAZEL

24

"Then there was Azazel," she said. She wasn't sure why she had suddenly thought of him, and yet the things he had done had affected her. The memory of him crashed over her, like a wave on a rough ocean.

"Tell us about Azazel," the Judge said. His stern gaze never once changed, and Isabella could feel his strong overview of all she was feeling, all she was remembering. What would Azazel add to this discussion? Isabella could not see it, but the Judge's insight was beyond her own understanding. Isabella also noticed that Theo had raised an eyebrow. He leaned forward as if he was about to say something, accuse her of something, even after all this time, but Sirius silenced him before he could say a word. "Go on."

"I first met Azazel at college, before I met Theo," she said, hoping that would be enough to prevent him from accusing her of anything, even though she had nothing to apologize for, least of all to him, and certainly not for Azazel. But slowly, the memory began to unfold.

Azazel had turned plenty of heads on the first day of college, sauntering in five minutes after their very first class had started, clearly determined to make an entrance. She remembered his Adonis-like form and searching eyes; his eyes were the first things you noticed before being completely captivated by the rest of his appearance. Broad-shouldered, sculpted, and self-assured, Azazel had the physique of an athlete. His hair was wild, his face pale, and his clothes flamboyant. A peacock. Several girls tried to make eye contact with him, hoping that he would take one of the empty seats near them, and a couple of boys did too. Isabella hoped that he wouldn't choose the seat next to her. Her disappointment grew when he did.

The teacher was unimpressed by his entrance as well, but Azazel seemed to win him over with his unconventional ideas about art, his knowledge of the latest trends, and his enthusiasm for the subject. He almost won Isabella over too, but she soon realized that her first impression had been accurate, and his constant need for attention became irritating.

It wasn't just in class. He would follow her to the cafeteria and insist on sitting with her, even though she tried her best to find a table that was already occupied. She attempted to discourage him, but no matter what she did, he always seemed to be around. He was pursuing her; his raw desire was impossible to conceal.

As the weeks went by and it became clear that she wouldn't be swayed by his charms, he turned his attention to one of the other girls, hoping to make her jealous, but his plan failed. He still made a point of examining Isabella's work, almost as if he were the authority in the room, but there was always praise woven into his indirect comments. Nevertheless, he was always there, peering over her shoulder as she worked, as if she were a student in his class.

He didn't make it through the second semester. The tutors grew weary of his antics, his tardiness, his excuses for incomplete assignments, and eventually, his discovery of smoking weed in the library. Isabella wasn't surprised, and if anything, she felt a slight sense of relief. She knew that many others smoked as well, and it wasn't as if she had never tried it herself, but several of them had taken it further. The difference was that they hadn't been caught.

In that final semester of her first year at college, it felt like a weight had been lifted from her shoulders. The tutors had been there to offer advice and make suggestions, but they didn't watch her while she worked unless she asked them to. There was freedom in what she was doing as she experimented, developing her own style. That was what led to her winning the prize; that is what had made her the artist she had become. It was the one thing she had that was truly hers.

By the time she returned for her second year, she had almost completely forgotten about Azazel. It wasn't until several years later that she saw him again but didn't recognize him at first.

She had been working in the gallery for some time, enjoying her work and responsibilities, when one morning she noticed a man who kept walking past, pausing at the window, and looking in without ever stepping inside. Many people did not notice the man as they were far less observant, whereas some of them didn't notice as they were simply distracted by work or their commute. Also, the man was not the only one taking an interest in Isabella's paintings from outside on the sidewalks; many others had this tendency to stop and admire some works without coming in.

Isabella liked to imagine that they had been captivated by a piece that could be seen from outside but never coming any closer because they knew they could not afford the price. At least they could enjoy it while it was still in the gallery. But this strange man was different. His hair was long, unkempt, and he had a ragged beard in desperate need of tidying up. He wore a long grey trench coat, even though the sun was shining. What was more disconcerting was that he wasn't looking at any of the pieces of art on display; he was looking at her, unblinking. It sent a shiver up her spine, but she tried to ignore him. She should have recognized him once she saw his eyes, but something about it had lost its youthful charm; it was darker and empty.

She made herself busy at the back of the shop, but whenever she glanced towards the window, he was still standing there, watching her as if nothing else mattered. The telephone rang, and she answered it, glad for the distraction. When the call finally ended, the man had gone. It was only when he appeared again the following morning that she suspected she knew who he was. She raised a slight smile and opened the door to him, part of her hoping that he would just walk away. Instead, he just stood there and smiled back.

"Azazel?" she said, but she no longer had any doubts that it was him. "What are you doing here?"

"I heard you were working here," he said. "Thought I'd drop by and say how proud I am of you."

"Proud? Why should you be proud?"

"Because of the prize you won. I was there, you know. Couldn't keep away."

She couldn't believe what he was saying. How did he manage to get in there? And why? He had been such a small part of the course, and little more than an irritant. Her success had nothing to do with him.

"Anyway," he said. "I'm glad I was able to help."

"Help? How did you help? What did you ever do apart from picking fault with what I was doing?"

He looked shocked. "All the advice I gave you at college."

"Advice?" She was doing her best to keep that familiar annoyance inside but felt she was failing. It was as if he had lived in a different world, one in which everyone looked up to him, whether they wanted to or not.

"It's okay," he said. "There's no need to thank me."

"You're right, there isn't because I have nothing to

thank you for." It was as if a dam had burst, and the things she had wanted to say back then came flooding out. Still, he looked surprised, affronted, and took a step back. Before she finished, he had turned and started to walk away, and for a moment she felt ashamed for having spoken to him that way. The truth was, she meant every word of it, but even after he had hurried around the corner, she was still angry and upset. Things were going right for her, and she really didn't need someone like Azazel coming along and spoiling things.

He didn't appear again for a couple of days, or at least she didn't notice him, but the next time he stood outside the gallery, she found herself shaking, trembling. He clearly wasn't taking no for an answer, and she didn't know how to deal with him. In the end, she didn't have to do anything. Vicky saw that she was upset and asked her what the trouble was, and Isabella told her the whole story. Vicky didn't hesitate to act. She strode to the door without pausing and flung it open forcefully. Isabella saw that it had startled Azazel, but nowhere near as much as the rant that Vicky launched herself into. Isabella could hear every word, even though she was in the rear of the gallery, and the street door had swung closed. Hell, the whole of the street must have been able to hear, especially her closing words. "If I see you around here again, I'll be calling the police."

Azazel tried to respond, though Isabella couldn't hear what he was saying. Vicky was having none of it. She simply came back inside the shop, allowing the door to swing shut on him. He must have known that there was nothing to be gained and had left. A wave of relief washed over Isabella, but she knew that she would still be looking over her shoulder wherever she went, just to make sure he wasn't there. He had gotten under her skin, and it would be a while before she got rid of that feeling completely.

CHAPTER EIGHT

NEW BEGINNINGS

♄

"At around that time, I received an invitation to the opening of a new hotel in London. At Vicky's insistence, whom I also considered a friend, I decided to attend. I didn't quite understand why she had insisted so much, she wanted to give me a chance to get away from the risk of bumping into Azazel. It had been a couple of weeks since I last saw him, but that didn't mean I had stopped looking out for him. Every time I saw someone who might have been him, my heart rate increased, and my legs felt weak. I had almost stopped going out in the evenings to avoid the possibility. It seemed better that way."

"It was at this hotel opening that I met Eaton for the first time, and my soul realized that he had something I was missing; a kind of feminine energy that did not seem out of place in him. It took a while, but eventually, I told myself that I could pursue my dreams with him, though he barely seemed to notice me."

Isabella felt that familiar uplifting, supportive feeling she had experienced in the pool again and understood what was happening to her. She fought against it for a moment, but then relaxed into it. She was reluctant for Theo to see her memories of things that had nothing to do with him, especially her happy memories, but he could not hurt her anymore. She hadn't cared about him knowing about Azazel, but that had been different. Azazel had been someone who had intruded in her life, not someone she had welcomed in.

"At the hotel opening, I was wearing a simple but elegant black dress which hugged my feminine frame in a modest yet tantalizing fashion. The ensemble was paired with a cherry scent, and only a light touch of makeup, but it was enough. My hair hung loose and casual. I might have looked like a confident woman, ready to take on the world, but inside me, I was as nervous as anything. The social terrain was still unfamiliar, and I was grateful to have Vicky there with me, helping me navigate it."

"Vicky, on the other hand, was dressed to the nines, full of life and seemed to know half of the people there, most of them raising a hand or a glass in acknowledgement when they made eye contact with her. I wished I could be more like her, comfortable as the center of attention, but for that night, I was comfortable walking in her steps."

"Eaton was attending to each table in turn, exuding charm and smiles. He possessed an outstanding presence, with his ingenuity and industry being well spoken of, so it came as no surprise to see heads turn as he walked by. He seemed brimming with energy. They had a brief conversation when he approached their table, ensuring they had everything they needed. I surmised that he had already uttered the same words a dozen times that evening and was only halfway through the room."

"We coincidentally met a few more times at events, mostly arranged by mutual acquaintances of Vicky and Eaton, and a friendship blossomed. There was even a point when I wondered if Vicky had orchestrated our encounters. Regardless of the truth behind it, I eventually managed to completely put Azazel out of my mind."

"In Eaton 's eyes, I saw a reflection of myself, akin to looking into a mirror and encountering something familiar. I perceived the sadness and worry that resided within me; there was a nervousness he struggled to conceal, as if he were weary of something, and it pained my soul."

"We got along very well as friends, gradually sharing our secrets and dreams, until I grew comfortable enough to confide in him about the affair with Madeline and how we had concealed it from her husband. He disclosed that he had experienced a similar situation with his flat mate, James. In fact, the shared experiences and similarities in our destinies further connected us. Besides his materialistic tendencies, he possessed the right spirit for me. We could engage in lengthy conversations, which was unusual for me as I wasn't typically talkative. Over time, Eaton began treating me like his girlfriend. He sent me flowers every day, providing a stark contrast to Theo; he was not manipulative but rather attentive and affectionate. It marked the first time in my life that I had received such an abundance of flowers. Neither Theo nor my father had ever bought me any. For a while, I felt like a princess."

"Eaton resembled the man of my dreams, and I never anticipated that this dream would end in disappointment." Isabella paused, experiencing a surge of profound tranquility reminiscent of her soul communicating with her. The message conveyed by Isabella's soul was that her feminine energy resided in Eaton 's body, while his masculine energy resided within her. They completed each other. Even in that courtroom, she was overwhelmed as she felt it again.

"You have done well, my child. Let us continue from here," welcomed Judge Sirius. Isabella's memories had not fully unraveled in her mind, allowing Theo and the judge to see through her mind's eye…

Things weren't always rosy for Isabella while with Eaton. Although Eaton was a wonderful man, he still had a troubling trait: Eaton liked to be in the spotlight and valued status and fame; appearances mattered a great deal to him. Isabella didn't appreciate this, but somehow, he managed to make her appear as though she enjoyed the same things when they started living their relationship publicly. It was as if they were each playing their roles, and she found herself behaving more and more like him.

While strolling in the park on a warm spring day, with trees resonating with birdsongs, Isabella noticed a woman stumbling and fainting a short distance ahead.

She quickened her pace as others rushed to help the woman. The fact that so many people stopped to assist was a testament to the kind spirit of Juan, but there needed to be balance in the universe. Some people merely glanced in the woman's direction and continued on their way, even tutting as if they believed she had brought her condition upon herself, inconveniencing them by daring to be unwell. Isabella overheard a pair of women making spiteful and condescending remarks about the woman drinking so early in the day.

Only as Isabella drew closer did she realize that the woman was her own mother. Several concerned individuals had already gathered around her, assisting her to a nearby bench. To avoid revealing her identity, Isabella ignored them and hurried past. The thought crossed her mind that her mother may have actually been drinking early that morning, and she was determined not to be embarrassed by her. Besides, her mother was already receiving help from plenty of people.

Upon arriving home, Isabella was astonished by her own behavior. She couldn't comprehend how she had become so indifferent and apathetic—but it was all Eaton 's fault. When she gazed into the mirror, she no longer recognized the woman staring back at her. Isabella realized she was becoming increasingly like him, and she hadn't even noticed until that moment. She made the decision to leave him that day, devastated by what was happening to her.

Eaton didn't object, which hurt, but Isabella was still content with her decision. However, a month later, she discovered that she was pregnant and didn't know what to do. The pregnancy was unplanned, and she wasn't sure if she was ready to have a baby, or if Eaton was ready either. She called Madeline, who suggested she should tell Eaton , but Isabella disagreed; she needed time to think about it first. Two or three days later, Eaton persistently called her, asking her to join him at the hotel restaurant for dinner.

"I think we need to talk," he said. He didn't specify the reason, and she didn't need to ask. She was already certain that Madeline would have informed him, and deep down, which was what she had hoped for when she had confided in her about the situation. It relieved her of the stress of having to initiate the conversation herself and allowed him time to contemplate. It was for the best. Isabella initially resisted the idea of meeting, but she knew he would persist and wouldn't give up until he achieved his desired outcome. The least she could do was engage in a discussion with him. She owed him that much, so they made arrangements to meet that evening.

It took Isabella some time to decide which dress to wear. By the time she reached a decision, her entire wardrobe was laid out on the bed. She opted for a dress she had purchased for herself rather than the one Eaton had bought her. It might not have been as glamorous as the others, but it expressed more about her true self than what he desired her to be. Her choice of dress was an act of empowerment.

Upon arriving at the hotel, she discovered that all of their friends were present. She was surprised but incredibly happy...

"Thank you," the Judge interrupted as Isabella snapped out of the relaxed state, she had immersed herself in. The moment she emerged from the water, that memory was sealed off from everyone else.

"I believe this demonstrates that life is replete with choices and opportunities to alter one's destiny. You could have chosen not to attend that meeting. You could have refused to meet Eaton and raised the child on your own. You could have even made the decision, like many young women in your situation, not to have the baby."

"I would never have considered that," Isabella snapped, shocked at the suggestion. Her facial expression contorted with anger, and her lower lip quivered slightly.

"I apologize," the Judge said. "I didn't mean to imply that you would, but it is crucial to acknowledge that it was a possibility available to you, yet you consciously decided against it. These are the choices that God presents to you."

"I didn't mean..."

"It doesn't matter," the Judge interjected. "Please continue."

This time, Isabella would conclude in her own words. "We got married, and eventually, I gave birth to a baby boy. We named him Sam," Isabella stated. "But before he turned one, a battle of egos began between Eaton and James. James had been grooming his own son, Vicente, to take over the business. Eaton saw it as a challenge, and in a way, it marked the beginning of the end for our relationship."

"Sometime later, James sold some of his shares to a young businesswoman named Demi. This further offended Eaton because both of his partners were now much younger than him, and they excluded him, believing he was less dynamic and productive. The situation enraged Eaton , and he took it out on me in various ways, but there was nothing I could do about it."

CHAPTER NINE

MOTHERHOOD

"Sam was a bit of a handful, but I suppose all babies can be. They are messy miracles that overhaul your life in the most chaotic beauty known to man. Eaton was so busy all the time that he wasn't around to help much. When he was, all he did was complain that the house wasn't clean enough, that I hadn't done his laundry, or that the food was not ready for him whenever he came home. Even if the food was ready, he would complain that he had eaten at the hotel. No matter what I did, it was never enough for him. Nothing was ever enough."

"Sam took up all of my time, demanding so much attention, and the only way I got any peace was by giving it. But that left no time for anything else. There was no time for housework, for cooking, for my friends... no time for me. It was only in warm weather when I could take him out for walks that I started to feel that I got even a moment to myself. After spending weeks cooped up with my son, taking care of him and failing at performing other wife duties, stepping out into fresh air and sunlight was a gust of relief."

"I used to take him to the park and sit with him while I fed the ducks. At that point, I was practically abandoned by most of my friends; no one wants to be tied down to helping out a nursing mother when they have their whole lives ahead of them. Sam was my only companion, and I would talk to him as I fed the ducks, and although he was too young to understand anything, I was content with his bubbling and cooing sounds. I also enjoyed seeing him so curious about the birds; he would reach out as if he could grab them, and I would relish the beauty of his daring endeavor. Sam would also clap his tiny hands in pure joy as the ducks splashed and flapped their wings, competing for the crumbs that I would scatter on the water's surface. He would laugh and smile when people looked into his pram. There seemed to be plenty of other mums in the same boat; I recognized the tired look on their faces."

"I should have been happy. I would lie in bed at night pleading and begging with my higher self to just be happy. I had brought this new life into the world, I was married to a man I thought I loved, and lived in the kind of house I had once dreamed of living in. Eaton worked hard, but he was doing it to provide for our future and I shouldn't really have had anything to complain about, but I was so exhausted all the time. When I told Eaton what the problem was... that I was having trouble managing everything... I expected him to explode. I thought he would be angry, but he wasn't. Somehow, he was incredibly calm. He was shown a problem and his instinct was to solve it."

"We'll hire a nanny," he said, simple as that. He had the magic wand and was able to wave it. I got the feeling that there should be a price to pay in time, and I guess, in a way, there was. But for now, he was giving me the opportunity to be the woman he wanted me to be. Whatever his motivation was, it didn't matter; things were going to get better. I wouldn't have been able to bear it if it got any worse.

"Within a couple of days, he'd found someone he said was suitable, and she had moved into the spare room. Magda was younger than me and effortlessly beautiful, no matter what she wore, while I felt tired and old. Magda radiated a glow and an aura of class with which I couldn't compete. It felt like having Sam had aged me by at least ten years.

I was shocked that he had made the decision without asking my opinion, without us even discussing the idea of her actually living with us. But when I raised the issue, he grew defensive, making it out that he had sorted my problem for me, that I should be grateful he had taken care of everything. But I didn't feel grateful, I didn't even feel angry. I felt numb. Looking back now, I'm not even sure why I would have been surprised if he had acted that way; he always did. I should have seen it as a sign."

"I have said before," Judge Sirius said when she paused for a moment, "that God sends signs, offers choices. He is giving you the opportunity to find the right path."

"I know," Isabella said. "But I just didn't see it at the time. I should have, but I didn't. All I could see was a way to stop feeling so tired all the time. I even thought I might be able to get back to my painting. I hadn't picked up a brush in months, not since Sam was born, and I was missing it. Maybe that was what had been making me feel so low. Maybe paint, for me, was like a drug, an addiction, and without it, I was lost."

She looked at Sirius again as if he might have something else to say, that he might agree with her or tell her that she was wrong, but he said nothing. The ball of light simply floated, shifting in the air only slightly, like a balloon on a taut string, its light softly increasing and decreasing in intensity, like some kind of pulse. She knew that he was waiting for her to say more, her story was incomplete.

"Eaton came home from work early that first week when Magda moved in with us, to find me in my studio in the attic. I hadn't been up there in so long, but I wanted to make the most of my newfound freedom. The house was spotless, Sam had been bathed and was ready to be put down in his cot, and dinner was almost ready. All of it was Magda's doing, of course. I had been up there for a few hours and had managed to lose myself in my art, creativity bursting out of me after being restrained for so long. I had been working for at least five hours, but the time had disappeared in the blink of an eye."

"I thought he would have been happy that I had found the time to do something for myself, and while he didn't say anything, I could tell that he was not particularly pleased. Over dinner, he told me how busy he had been at work and about the challenges that his new, younger partners were causing him. I tried to be supportive, but it seemed he wanted more than words, even though he didn't say so that evening."

"I didn't go back into my studio the next day, or for the rest of the week, feeling guilty about being able to spend time doing what made me happy while Eaton was working harder than ever. When I suggested that we find time to do something over the weekend he snapped at me, telling me that he couldn't afford to take the time off when he had so much to do at work. I asked if there was anything I could do to help, anything that might take some of the weight off him. I half expected him to say no, but instead he welcomed my offer. Over the next weeks and months, I did more for the business, and the new painting I had started was left unforgotten in my attic studio—simply discarded and left to rot."

CHAPTER TEN

MOTHER AND DAUGHTER

"I was also neglecting my mother and father. I heard that my father was getting remarried; he had chosen my mother's birthday for his wedding day. Her friends had told my mother, who usually called me every Sunday, but she did not call that week. Before that, I wouldn't have been concerned; it wasn't that unusual for her to forget, but I had a strange feeling inside. As it was the day before her birthday, I thought I'd go and wish her Happy Birthday a day early. I took her a bunch of flowers, but when I knocked on the door, she didn't open it. I was concerned, so I used my spare key and went inside. I called out, but still didn't get an answer. I went into the living room and found my mother lying on the sofa with her wrists slashed, blood everywhere. I stared at the blood on the floor for a few minutes, unable to accept the situation, and couldn't even bring myself to get close to her. At that moment, I created a stage for myself in my head, a scenario I wanted to believe in. I opened the windows; I wanted to live the moment for the last time."

"Then I started to make cupcakes for her. I lit a candle, and then, as I approached my mother towards the end of this daydream, I returned to the real world, crying, 'Come on, Mum, blow the candle out.' I took her in my arms like a baby and started to cry, a pain stabbing deep inside me. My mother had ended her own life out of love for my father."

"They had a toxic relationship, but I had never thought she would do that. I was angry that she had fallen in love so stupidly, but I was no different from her in experiencing deep feelings. I didn't see my father after that day. His wedding went ahead as planned, despite what had happened, but a few months later, he had a heart attack and died. Everything came together, overwhelming me, and I couldn't handle so much sadness."

"I decided to visit Madeline for comfort. She received me warmly, held my hands, and offered her support, but when she went up the stairs for some reason, I took drugs from her medicine cabinet to blot away the pain. I was desperate for anything to numb my sorrow. On this unfortunate day, I overdosed and was in the hospital when I opened my eyes. Madeline and Eaton were at my bedside, softly calling my name. I took a deep breath. I didn't remember what had happened at first, but then it all came back to me: the pain, the drugs, and the moment of relief when I had started to slip away. It was like I had been born for a second time. In a moment of weakness, I lost myself and realized that what I had done was wrong for so many reasons."

"People around me always used to say that I was strong, a word I hated because I wanted to be happy, not strong, like in fairy tales. But life is not a fairy tale; I understand that now. My soul was beginning to be enlightened; it was not yet time for me to go."

"Eaton was angry with me, but he was hiding it inside him. Madeline was crying, happy that I had woken up. I was discharged and allowed to go home, but Eaton did not talk to me all the way back. At home, I was touched when I saw my son, and I hugged him tightly. He was completely unaware of the situation, though Magda had been taking good care of him."

"I hadn't given him a second thought when I had been taking those pills, and I hated myself for it."

Eaton and I went to the bedroom, and his expression suddenly changed. He told me that I was not to see Madeline again, and I reacted very badly."

"I always respected your relationship with James," I said. "I knew that you were more than just friends, but not once did I say that I didn't want there to be three people in this relationship because I loved you and respected you. I turned a blind eye to your behavior, and now you cannot interfere with what I do. Madeline was in my life before you, and she always will be."

"Eaton was very angry, but he did not react in a dramatic way, perhaps because there was no one else who could support him. James, the one he had always trusted the most when we first met, had always been determined to break us up."

"Love is a beautiful feeling, Isabella," the Judge said. "Man was created with love and affection."

"Yes," Isabella replied. "But I never found it. The last painting, I made was called 'The Shattered Angel,' and it became the target of religious imagery. In the painting, I depicted an angel descending from the bright sky, being destroyed by the people waiting for it on the ground."

"What did you want to say in that picture, Isabella?"

"That God loves man unconditionally, but he is offended because they are cruel. Evil or heartless people destroyed the angel sent for their salvation, even though tears were flowing from their eyes. Man is eaten up by his own wickedness. He constantly roars and moves about perpetuating evil. He can't help it; instead, he tries to hide his wretchedness inside him, but unfortunately, his cruelty cannot be stopped."

"Christian Faith says Man was expelled from paradise as the price for eating the forbidden fruit. The people I painted do not act that way because they were expelled from paradise, but because they couldn't steal what they saw there."

"My relationship with Eaton was deteriorating. Every person has a dark side, but I accepted that he was a materialist, money-loving, ambitious person. I tried to be there for him and accept him as he was, though it was difficult. It was as if a monster had emerged from where it had been hiding in him. He was trying to shape me, turn me into the woman he wanted me to be, rather than the woman I was. Not only that, but I also thought he wanted me to be involved in the business, to help him carry some of the weight. I soon realized that this was not the truth; he wanted me there so he could gain some balance with his younger partners. In so many ways, he was just using me. I couldn't get used to the rapid pace of this life; it wasn't me. My job was to dream, to create, and to do that, I needed peace. But my soul was in turmoil."

Theo interrupted with a queasy smirk. "This is probably what the modern Beauty and the Beast is like." The joke was not taken lightly.

"It is not a laughing matter, Theo," the Judge warned in a serious voice, his gaze laser-focused on Theo, under which Theo squirmed. "Please go ahead, Isabella."

She nodded. "You are right, Judge," Isabella said. "I see now that there were similarities between the way Theo and Eaton treated me."

"My eyes were hollow, tired, and itchy from reading all the documents he had given me and the list of tasks I needed to take care of at the hotel. And when I got back home, I had to tell Eaton what had happened. He would want to know everything. He was filling my head with information as if I were a boxer, and he was preparing me for a match. It was relentless, and I didn't know how long I could deal with it."

"I was tired one evening when the inspiration for the painting came. I was going to paint in a way that would make everyone wonder what the artist had been taking."

"I couldn't remember how long it had been since I was last in my studio. I couldn't even be sure if I had been up there since that afternoon when Magda had first joined us. Back then, Sam had been less than six months old, but now he was a little boy rather than a baby. When I got up there, though, I was shocked to find that Eaton had filled the room with boxes, taking up so much of the space that was supposed to be mine. It was as if I was blinded; the disruption destroyed my concentration. Angrily, I went downstairs to confront him about it."

"Eaton said that he did it so that I would focus on my work at the hotel, the work that I had offered to do to share some of the burden he was carrying. He told me to wake up, not to daydream in the bubble I had made in my head. At least that was the way he saw things; that I was just wrapped up in myself and what I wanted to do."

"He had no respect for me or my work. Whenever there was a discrepancy that fell within my jurisdiction, he would throw me to the wolves, holding me accountable in front of his partners whenever I failed, as if I were one of his employees. He also barely offered me encouragement when I succeeded, only concentrating on my shortcomings. I had no choice but to be strong."

CHAPTER ELEVEN

VICENTE

P

"I was spending more time at the hotel and less at home. Magda was spending more time with Sam than I was with him. I worried that my son would forget what his parents looked like since he was becoming so used to her glamorous smile and smooth complexion. I had to go into work early, sometimes before Eaton , and occasionally worked longer than he did if he had to attend a meeting somewhere where I was not needed. I started to long for more time with Sam, no matter how tired I had been."

"When the never-ending work started to take its toll, I began to take a walk at lunchtime rather than working through it while I ate a sandwich at my desk. On the days when the weather was fine, I would grab a coffee and sit in the park, often on the bench near the lake where Sam and I had fed the ducks. I saw the new mothers enjoying their time with their babies and young children, filling the air with laughter. Somehow, even that had been taken from me."

"Usually when I sat on that bench, I was left alone, occasionally getting a smile from the mothers passing by, without ever striking up a conversation. But one day, that changed."

Isabella now felt that familiar change starting to come upon her, and she knew that the moment was about to be shared. She had nothing to hide, and this was her opportunity to prove it. Isabella closed her eyes and felt the sun on her face, heard the excited chatter of young children and the quacking of ducks, and if she breathed in deeply, she caught the smell of newly mown grass. Even with her eyes closed, she would have known where she was and what time of year. This bench had become her special place, her escape, for half an hour a day whenever she could. It was her escape.

"Hello there," a voice said, bringing her out of her moment of peace. She opened her eyes, blinking against the sun, and looked at the owner of the voice. She blinked twice before she realized who it was.

"Vicente," she said. She saw James' son most days in the hotel, but they rarely spoke. She was mostly left to do relatively menial or routine jobs that kept her occupied, unable to think of anything other than what was in front of her.

"You were miles away," he said, joining her on the bench without being invited. "Everything alright?"

"Fine," she said. "Just taking a few minutes before I head back."

"He works you too hard," the young man said, flashing a warm commiserating smile at her.

"Just doing my share," she said. "We all have to pitch in, don't we?"

"I guess," he said. "But there might be a better use for your skills. My dad tells me you're a painter, and a good one at that."

She smiled, surprised that James was even aware of what she did, let alone that he had told his son. Why would he? She hoped the smile was enough.

"Maybe we could get some of your art on display in the hotel, have an exhibition. It might be good for both the hotel and your work."

"The hotel is my work now. I haven't painted anything new in a while. Certainly not enough to put a show together."

"That's a shame. We should find a way to make more time for you to paint. I'll speak to Eaton about it."

"No," she said, a little too quickly. "Please don't."

"Okay," he said, a look of disappointment on his face. "Let me know if you change your mind."

He left her then, and all she could think about was what she had lost. But then the moment was over, and her memory jumped a few hours. She was now at home before Eaton , not having seen him all afternoon, and when he came in, he was clearly angry.

"How long has it been going on?" he demanded.

"How long has what been going on?"

"You and Vicente. How long has it been going on?" His face was growing red, his temper barely restrained.

"Nothing's going on with Vicente, or anyone else," Isabella said. "Nothing." He slammed his furious palm on the table, rattling the cutlery and almost overturning a wine glass. A splash of red stained the white tablecloth, slowly spreading. She started to get up to fetch a cloth.

"Leave it," he said. "I want the truth. Now."

"That is the truth," she insisted. "Why won't you believe me?"

"Because you were seen, in the park, all cozy together! Then he calls me and says that it would be a great idea if we had some of your art hanging in the hotel. Now where do you think he got an idea like that from?"

"From his father!" she snapped. She had never spoken to him in that tone before, nor had she seen the look of shock on his face that followed.

"What?"

She told him all about sitting on that park bench, about Vicente approaching her, and his idea. "He said he was going to leave it to me to talk to you about it if I thought it, was a good idea."

"And do you really think it's a good idea?"

"No, I don't," she said. "Not at the moment, at least. I don't have enough unsold work, and I don't have the time to create anything new. And I don't have the studio space if I did!"

Isabella was angry when the memory ended, and she became aware of being in the courtroom again, but no one said anything. Her lower lip was trembling again, but she found her calm and went on to say, "There were other times, more accusations," she said. "But there was never anything for him to be jealous about."

"So why do you think he was jealous if you gave him no cause?" the Judge asked, but Isabella simply shook her head.

"Maybe he was just accusing you of something that he was guilty of himself," Theo suggested. "Maybe he had a thing for this Magda. Whether there was anything going on between them or not, if you were seeing this guy, you'd be giving him the okay to do the same."

Isabella shook her head, though she was surprised at his insight. Was it possible that he was right? Might he have been looking for an excuse to make his move, or had there already been something going on between them? "Is that what you would have done?" she asked calmly.

"I might have," he admitted after a pause.

"Did you ever do it when we were together?" She wondered just how many times she might have been betrayed in her life, but this time he replied without hesitation.

"No. I never accused you of sleeping with other men, and you know it. You know that there were other women, but I never blamed you for it."

She looked at the Judge, but he said nothing. Had they not been in this place where there was nothing but the truth, he would have said something if Theo was lying. She had no reason not to believe him. A sense of vulnerability flooded Isabella because the truth, no matter how good, can be incredibly disarming.

CHAPTER TWELVE

A MISUNDERSTANDING CORRECTED

"After a while," she continued after a pause, "The news that Eaton had lung cancer only made things worse, and I wondered just how long he had known. Eventually, he could not even stand up, and his treatment continued in bed, with regular trips to the hospital. It was a very difficult time."

"At that time, I was focused on the work I needed to do for the hotel. Eaton called his closest friend, Arthur, to help me out at the hotel. Although, I didn't know whether it was to help me or control me. Eaton had him following me around, watching me, suspicious of everyone and everything, and no doubt reporting back to my husband."

"I never liked Arthur from the first time I met him. He had a callous roughness about him. His hair was a matted mess at the edges, and his collar was never folded in properly. He rarely smiled, not even when he was passing pleasantries. He had a stalking gait and a gruffness about the way he spoke; he sounded like someone who had not had a lot of love in his own life. He was supposed to be a support, but his very presence was antagonistic and accusing."

"After a while, he started living with us, frequently going in and out of the bedroom to talk to Eaton . Whenever he came down to dinner, he would sit in Eaton 's place, which was offensive and would always spoil my appetite. On one such night when he joined us for dinner, I left the table as I usually did and put Sam to bed early. Only Magda ate anything that evening, and she fell ill shortly after eating."

"Once this happened, I immediately went to Eaton and told him that I was suspicious of Arthur. But later, Arthur helped me with both the doctors and the business, and I regretted doubting him. I'm not sure how I would have managed without him being there." Isabella finished, but she was not fulfilled; she wasn't sure her testimony resolved her questions about the difficulty of that time in her life.

"What do you remember of the moment of your accident, Isabella?" the Judge asked.

"I remember I was driving fast. I remember being so eager to go faster that I pushed the car towards two hundred, and I kept looking up at the rearview mirror, right until I made a sharp blind bend, straight into the path of an incoming car. I swerved to the right to avoid hitting the car and drove straight into a tree. The impact knocked every bone in my body. It felt like I was a rag doll that had been jostled violently. I think some bones in my ribs fractured as the airbag stuffed my face, and the seatbelt nearly strangled me. I also felt excruciating pain that knifed through my thigh and immediately knocked me out. I wish I had stayed knocked out for long, for when I woke up, I almost wished I had died. I remembered that at the moment of impact, I could only picture Sam's face, and when I regained consciousness, the first and only thing I felt was pain; pain was everywhere, screaming through my senses, I really could not focus on anything else. I couldn't move my legs, and when I tried to make them budge, which rooted pain would make my head swoon. I think God saw my plight and tried to be merciful to me, for a few minutes in that hell was enough to take me out a second time. That's all I remember."

"Do you remember why you were driving so fast, Isabella?" said the Judge.

"I don't. It doesn't mean anything to me now. In my final days, I was in a void. Somehow, I knew that death was not far away. I had been poisoned, but not enough to make me seriously unwell. Perhaps I was trying to get myself to the hospital."

The Judge remained silent for a moment, as if contemplating something. He bowed his head for a minute, considering something that was not accessible to both souls. But Isabella sensed that what he was about to say held great insight.

"While I understand your reason for not being concerned about what caused your accident and the end of your life, it might be helpful to you when you depart from this place."

"If you believe it will be of assistance, then certainly, I will do as you suggest. But may I ask why you think it will help?"

"It would be better if there were no misunderstandings about what you believe led to the end of your life. It is better for you to know the truth, rather than holding the wrong person responsible."

"I understand," she said, allowing the memory to reveal itself to her.

She sat behind the wheel of her car, driving along familiar streets. The wipers intermittently cleared light drizzle from the windscreen. Every now and then, she glanced in her rear-view mirror, aware of a small red car. She remembered the initial apprehension and the slow creeping of raw fear as that car followed her for three turns and a considerable distance. The driver made no effort to catch up with her initially, but with every turn, the car drew a little closer. Until it was too close.

She pressed the accelerator, pushing the car slightly faster than the speed limit, hoping to put some distance between herself and the car behind. However, her effort made no difference. The other car also accelerated, then pulled out to overtake her. She eased off a bit, willing to let it pass, but it didn't speed away. Instead, it pulled alongside her, matching her speed.

She tightened her grip on the wheel and glanced at the other driver, hoping to understand their intentions, and she froze. She recognized the other driver, but it was the last person she had expected to see. She wouldn't have thought of him in a million years.

It was Azazel, after all this time. Azazel.

For a moment, fear surged through her, but it quickly gave way to something else. Anger. She was not going to be afraid of him anymore. She pressed the accelerator to the floor, and the car shot forward, leaving Azazel's car behind. She knew these roads well, certainly better than Azazel, but that wasn't enough. She took a bend too fast, just as a lorry came from the other direction, occupying the middle of the road, its horn blaring. She swerved and braked simultaneously, battling with the steering wheel, only for the rubber of her tires to slide on the slick asphalt. The car skidded off the road and onto the grass, spinning out of control. There was no stopping it. And then there was the tree.

So, it had nothing to do with Eaton .

"What happened to Azazel?" she asked the judge as she shook off the memory.

"His obsession with you had gotten the better of him," Judge Sirius said. "He had seen your picture in the newspaper and discovered where you were working. He even followed you home one evening, still desperately longing to be part of your life. He didn't intend to harm you; I am certain of that. He called for the emergency services and stayed with you until they arrived."

CHAPTER THIRTEEN

THE FINAL TESTIMONY

"There is one last testimony we need to hear," the Judge said. "We need to hear from someone whose soul is not yet due to be before this court for their own judgment but may have something important to say."

Both Isabella and Theo looked puzzled, their brows raised, and their lips curled in curiosity. They turned to each other in the hope that they might have some sort of answer. They did not have to wait long to discover what the Judge was referring to. The witness sitting behind Isabella, who had disguised himself as her father, rose to his feet and cast the blue and green powders into the air, just like before. His transformation was still taking place as he moved to stand in front of them, his back to the two souls being judged as he took his position.

As he turned, his shape changed, shrinking so that the cloak crumpled to a heap around him, revealing what he had become. The sight drew a sharp intake of breath from Isabella. Rather than the menacing figure he had been, he was now a small boy dressed in shorts and a T-shirt.

"Sam!" Isabella said, trying to get to her feet, but the chair wound its tentacles around her tightly.

"The boy is not here," the Judge reminded her, raising a gentle hand to pull her attention away from Sam. "This is simply a representation of your son, just as was the case with your father and Theo's mother. His spirit might not be here, but I have listened to his thoughts, and I know that what you are about to hear is the truth. It may also offer you comfort."

She was able to raise her hand and use a knuckle to wipe away a tear from her eyes.

"Mummy loved me very much," the boy began. It was his voice, Sam's voice. There was no mistaking it. It was the sweet coo of a child who had been the center of his mother's indulgence. "I have a nanny who looked after me, but it was Mummy who loved me, it was Mummy I called out for when I woke up from a bad dream. I wish she would come back."

"What about your father?" the Judge asked.

The boy seemed unfazed by the Judge's appearance, but Isabella had to remind herself that this wasn't actually her son. This was simply one of the cloaked figures who had taken his shape, his face, his voice.

"He's always in bed, and his health fails him, so he is too sickly to play with me. There is only me and Magda now. I don't think Daddy's going to get better, is he? I wish Mummy were here. She would make everything alright."

That was all he had to say. He reached down and pulled the gown back around him, pulled the hood over his head, and slowly grew to fill it. He was no longer the boy but the faceless figure there to witness proceedings. Without making another sound, he returned to his seat.

The Judge waited for a moment before speaking. "I think this says much about your final years, Isabella. There is no doubt that your son loved you, and at no point did he feel that you had neglected him. While he will miss your presence, he will remember you with only love and affection. There can be no doubt that you have learned much in this courtroom."

"I have listened to both of you. I believe you have found the answers to all your questions. The knowledge of your karmic lessons has been revealed today. And if you wish to learn, it will stay with you forever. The words of wisdom were passed through our conversations. The time to finish our session has arrived. We will see if this ending will give us a new beginning."

The verdict was about to be returned to the souls, but in the meantime, the room was filled with the soft, whispery sound of a flute. The melody started somewhere high up in the ceiling and echoed down to the few who were able to hear it. Again, like the strong hearty embrace they had felt with the Judge's first appearance, this flute was whispering to their Pneumas, urging them to accept their destiny.

"This is our farewell," said the Judge in a ceremonial tone to match his robes and grand charisma. "We should say goodbye to each other. It has been decided that Isabella has completed her spiritual journey, but Theo is to be given another chance to apply the knowledge he has learned during this hearing. However, Isabella has the power to save Theo from this journey if she wishes."

"You have the option, Isabella, to return to Earth, to meet Theo again, and help him complete his spiritual journey."

Theo glanced at Isabella and looked at her so intensely that she could almost feel it. His eyes were searing imaginary holes into the side of her face. He wanted her to seize the opportunity, and his will was so passionate that she felt compelled to help him. She was certain that he wanted them to be together on Earth, but this time the choice was hers, and he couldn't influence it.

Isabella looked at Theo with a mixture of pity and love. When she gazed into his eyes, this was nothing new for her. She had looked into those eyes hundreds of times before, but from his current position—begging, needy, and hoping that he would make a decision that considered her—Isabella was shocked to see how tired his eyes were. She had seen them filled with love and bitterness. She had seen them angry and scowling, but she had never seen them so deeply and emotionally exhausted. They were full of tears, yet at the same time, they were pleading for an answer.

After the briefest hesitation, Isabella replied, "I must admit that it is painful to realize that living with you was torment, just as it became with Eaton . Thus, my choice is made. Now, allow me to say it the way you would. My answer is the same as the last text you sent me. Goodbye, Theo!"

She uttered the words and instantly felt a sense of peace. Theo was no longer worth it; she would not dishonor all the effort she had put into regaining herself by returning to her tormentor. The Judge had stated that he had not attained spiritual enlightenment, despite having Isabella's unwavering affection and support, even at her own expense of suffering and isolation. Theo had turned a deaf ear even in this realm, despite experiencing the consequences of their lives. Never again. Isabella refused to look at him; in her eyes, he was now beneath her. Let someone else rehabilitate him, she thought.

Immediately after these words, the floor beneath Theo's feet caved in and sucked him into a black abyss. There was not a trace of him remaining, even though he had been sitting there just moments ago. His soul had been reincarnated back into the earthly realm. One of the witnesses who had been sitting behind him opened a ledger, made an entry, and closed it again. A judgment was made; a verdict recorded.

"Now tell me, my child, what does heaven look like to you?" asked the Judge.

Isabella was saddened but at peace. She had been torn for only a heartbeat over her decision about Theo. She had felt pity for him and briefly considered giving the answer he wanted. But she had endured enough pain at the hands of men and did not want to put herself through it again. It was her time now to enjoy the reward for the way she had lived her life.

She took a long pause to imagine her heaven before beginning to describe it. "I want to live in a log house somewhere surrounded by a snowy forest and watch the snow fall through the window. I want to see snowflakes falling peacefully outside my window, covering everything in feathery white snow. I want to experience this in the countryside and see capped mountains in the distance, where the Sun hides from view. When spring arrives, I want to sing and ride my bike so fast that even the wind won't be able to catch me. Or I just want to be a butterfly, surrounded by the scent of flowers and nature. Or a rain cloud that sheds its droplets down to Earth, to keep the soil irrigated. I still want to visit my son and protect him, whispering to him because I want him to grow up full of love. He needs a mother's love to become merciful and learn how to respect women. Women are the power of life on Earth."

The lights went out, and the court was adjourned. The souls had received their verdicts. The Judge heard the sound of a baby crying and opening its eyes to meet the world's light for the first time, beginning its journey of learning life's lessons. Vague shapes and snippets of words still lingered in the baby's memory. His mother had given birth to him in a prison, cuffed to a harsh, metal bed. An old soul had entered a new cycle of karma. For him, the race had begun. Again.

Printed in Great Britain
by Amazon

26371337R00106